Plain Language, Please

Plain Language, Please
How to Write for Results

Janet Arrowood

ROWMAN & LITTLEFIELD
Lanham • Boulder • New York • London

Published by Rowman & Littlefield
A wholly owned subsidiary of The Rowman & Littlefield Publishing Group, Inc.
4501 Forbes Boulevard, Suite 200, Lanham, Maryland 20706
www.rowman.com

Unit A, Whitacre Mews, 26-34 Stannary Street, London SE11 4AB

Copyright © 2016 by Janet C. Arrowood

All rights reserved. No part of this book may be reproduced in any form or by any electronic or mechanical means, including information storage and retrieval systems, without written permission from the publisher, except by a reviewer who may quote passages in a review.

British Library Cataloguing in Publication Information Available

Library of Congress Cataloging-in-Publication Data
Names: Arrowood, Janet C., author.
Title: Plain language, please : how to write for results / Janet C. Arrowood.
Description: Lanham : Rowman & Littlefield, [2016]
Identifiers: LCCN 2016015190 (print) | LCCN 2016026466 (ebook) |
   ISBN 9781475824759 (cloth : alk. paper) | ISBN 9781475824766 (pbk. : alk. paper) |
   ISBN 9781475824773 (Electronic)
Subjects: LCSH: English language—Rhetoric—Handbooks, manuals, etc. |
   English language—Grammar—Handbooks, manuals, etc. | Report writing—
   Handbooks, manuals, etc.
Classification: LCC PE1408 .A74 2016 (print) | LCC PE1408 (ebook) | DDC
   808/.042—dc23
LC record available at https://lccn.loc.gov/2016015190

∞™ The paper used in this publication meets the minimum requirements of American National Standard for Information Sciences—Permanence of Paper for Printed Library Materials, ANSI/NISO Z39.48-1992.

Printed in the United States of America

Contents

Preface		vii
Introduction		ix
1	A Brief History of the (American) English Language	1
2	How to Write in Plain English	5
3	Identify and Write to the "Right" Audience	7
4	Keep It Simple and Short	11
5	Planning and Organizing Your Documents	31
6	Applying the "Cs" and Rs" of Effective Writing	37
7	Using Correct Grammar and Punctuation	47
8	Using Reader-Friendly Voice, Tone, and Person	65
9	Applying Effective Self-Editing and Self-Proofreading Techniques	69
10	Netiquette and Writing for the Likely Viewing Medium	73
Conclusion: The Wrap-Up		79
About the Author		81

Preface

The world is filled with English grammar books, self-help books about writing, and style guides, so why write another "English" book? Simply put, there really aren't any books that explain the whys, whats, and hows of writing using plain language.

Writing is an essential skill in the workplace. It doesn't matter if you are an engineer, nurse, government employee, scientist, welder, teacher, student, and so forth. If you can't write clearly and concisely, in plain English, your message may never get through. If you want someone to do something, or respond to something, your message must be obvious during the first reading. Busy people rarely have the time or inclination to read something a second time.

For over fifteen years, I've been developing and presenting training programs about the practicalities of effective writing. The participants include people in administrative, professional, technical, and skilled trades from corporations, governments, associations, and other organizations. No one is exempt from a need to communicate effectively, in the clearest, simplest terms possible. Unfortunately, writing using plain language—in plain English—is not a skill that is often taught. It must be learned "on the job," but there is rarely someone with the necessary skills to convey this critical training.

This book takes the materials, methods, and approaches I've developed and honed over more than thirty years as a professional writer, editor, and trainer of writers and puts them into an easy-to-follow format. The principles of plain language are explained and demonstrated. By following nine simple steps, you can become a much better writer and your writing will get the results you need.

Good writers are made, not born.

Introduction

Why write a book about "writing in plain English"? Simple. Because businesses and government are increasingly emphasizing the need to write using "plain English" or "plain language."

Why write in plain English? The clearer and more concise your writing is, the more likely you are to get the responses and results you want. Consider the comparisons given in table I.1.

Table I.1 Clear versus Turgid Writing: Responses

Well-written documents—documents written in plain English—enable your readers to:	Poorly written, turgid, text-dense documents encourage your readers to:
Read what you write	Avoid reading what you write
Quickly understand what you write and what you are trying to accomplish—what you want from the reader	Misunderstand or misinterpret what you are trying to accomplish
Remember you, and your organization, favorably	Think about you, and your organization, unfavorably

Writing well—clearly, concisely, plainly, and in an audience-friendly style—is a science that anyone can learn.

Even the Federal Government is getting involved: In 2010, President Obama signed the Plain Writing Act (figure I.1). The act was modified and expanded in 2011.[1]

Yes, the Plain Writing Act applies to the Federal Government, and not the local or state governments or corporate and nongovernmental workplaces. But the act has some beneficial applications to anything any of us writes.

PUBLIC LAW 111–274—OCT. 13, 2010   124 STAT. 2861

Public Law 111–274
111th Congress

An Act

To enhance citizen access to Government information and services by establishing that Government documents issued to the public must be written clearly, and for other purposes.

Oct. 13, 2010
[H.R. 946]

Be it enacted by the Senate and House of Representatives of the United States of America in Congress assembled,

Plain Writing Act of 2010.
5 USC 301 note.

SECTION 1. SHORT TITLE.

This Act may be cited as the "Plain Writing Act of 2010".

SEC. 2. PURPOSE.

5 USC 301 note.

The purpose of this Act is to improve the effectiveness and accountability of Federal agencies to the public by promoting clear Government communication that the public can understand and use.

Figure I.1 **The Plain Writing Act of 2010.** *Source*: U.S. Public Law 111-274 October 13, 2010.

The clearer and simpler your message is, the more likely readers are to read it, understand it, and act on it in the way you intended.

So, why would you want to write in plain English? Here are three compelling reasons.

First, English is the "common" language in many places in the world. It is the language used in international activities by businesses, the aviation industry, organizations, governments, and travelers, as well as many sites on the Internet. But it is the second (or third, or fourth) language for many people.

Second, while English is the language learned by most of us, too often we avoid writing once we finish school. We watch videos. We write in social media slang and technical jargon. Sadly, the average person tends to read at a fifth- to sixth-grade level if he or she has finished high school, and this only rises to the ninth- to eleventh-grade level with a college diploma. Within someone's field of expertise, reading ability rises dramatically, regardless of the education level; but on a day-to-day basis, people prefer the language of journalism—the newspaper or stories and videos on the Web—to

The Economist magazine or professional journals. We want our information to come in short, simple, easy-to-follow sound bites, not text-dense paragraphs consisting of thirty-word sentences and ten-sentence paragraphs.

Finally, and most importantly, in a world so dependent on electronic communications, it is essential that meanings be clear and writing be concise. The clearer and more concise your writing is, the more likely you are to be understood and your words interpreted as you intended.

NOTE

1. http://www.plainlanguage.gov/plLaw/index.cfm.

Chapter 1

A Brief History of the (American) English Language

A BRIEF HISTORY OF ENGLISH

What makes English such a challenge to learn? Simply put, English evolved through "language thievery." If English speakers like a word, they take it. This tendency, combined with the vagaries of how these words are spelled and pronounced, has led to a language with more words than almost any other.

How did English evolve into its present form? There were many influences, and the language continues to evolve. The underlying root of English is the Anglo-Saxon dialects, but these evolved from other Germanic languages, as shown in figure 1.1.[1]

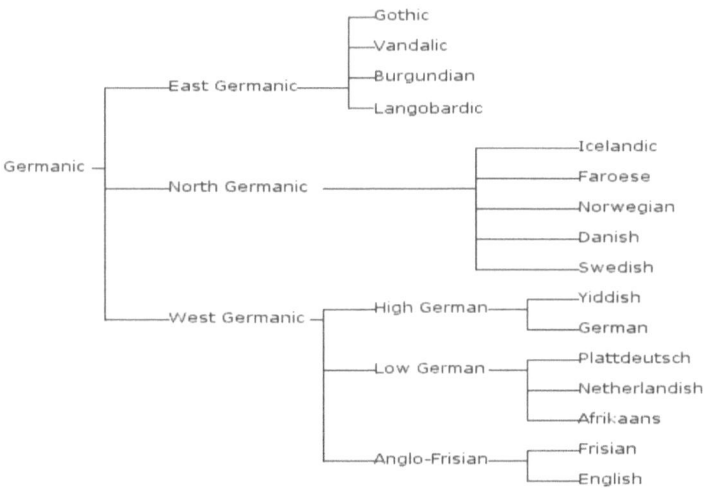

Figure 1.1   Germanic Language Tree

Over time, English continued to be influenced by invasions and conquests, especially the Vikings or Northmen (mostly Danish and Norwegian) in the ninth century and William the Conqueror from Normandy (English who fled the Viking conquest) in 1066.

The return of these "Normans" (from "Northmen") brought many French words and terms into English. French words formed the backbone of "educated" English—in fact, many of our scientific and lengthier words are directly recognizable in French. Most English words that end in -tion, -ence, and -ure are virtually identical in spelling and meaning with their French

Table 1.1 Linguistic Sources of Common English Words

Common Word (Germanic)	Wealthy Word (French)
Cow (German Kuh)	Beef (French Boeuf)
House (German Haus)	Mansion (French Maison)
Small or Short (German Kurtz)	Small (French Petit/Petite)

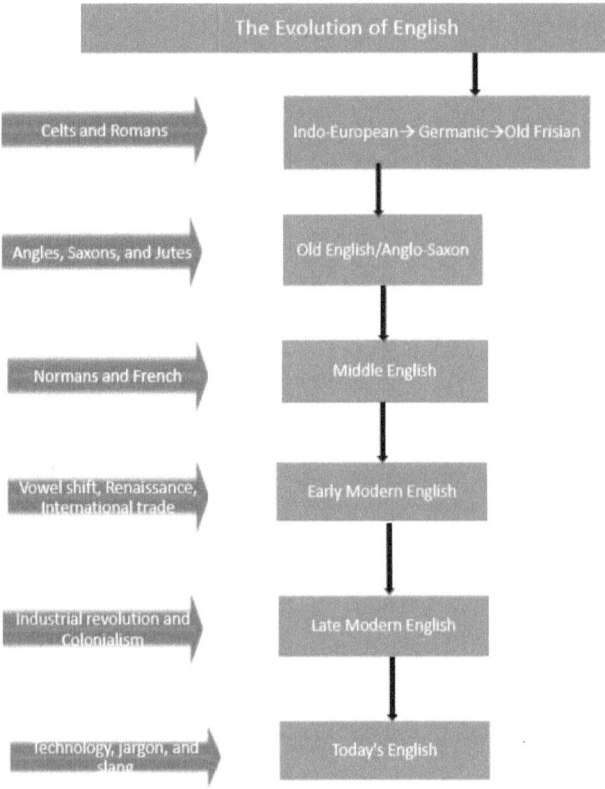

Figure 1.2 The Evolution of English

counterparts. It's thanks to the Normans we count the way we do: twenty-four rather than "four-and-twenty blackbirds baked into a pie. . . ."

On the other hand, many of our day-to-day words are readily identifiable with their Germanic/Anglo-Saxon sources: haus/house, kuh/cow, hund/hound, and katz/cat, for example.

Norman French became the language of the wealthy landowners, merchants, and such, while the Germanic/Anglo-Saxon language was used by the farmers, laborers, and so forth. This was one of the main ways English grew since there were two or more words for everything: the wealthy word and the poor word. Table 1.1 provides some examples of these word pairs.

Figure 1.2 gives a general idea of the main influences that created the English we speak today.

JUST HOW "BIG" IS ENGLISH, ANYWAY?

English is one of the three "biggest" languages in terms of total words. Exactly how many words are in three of the most widely spoken languages? Nobody seems to know for sure, but table 1.2 provides some estimates.

Table 1.2   Language/Approximate Number of Words

Language	~Number of Words	Words Needed in Daily Life
English*	~470,000* to over 1,000,000	~2,000 to 10,000
Chinese**	~100,000 to 370,000	~1,000 to 3,500 characters
Spanish***	~83,431	~1,000 to 10,000

*Webster's Third New International Dictionary Unabridged.
**Various English-Chinese dictionaries/Comprehensive Chinese Word Dictionary/Chinese News.
***DRAE (dictionary of the Spanish-language regulatory authority).

THE RISE OF ENGLISH AS A GLOBAL LANGUAGE

Why is English so widely spoken today? It's mostly a case of being in the right places at the right times. In the modern era, almost every major wave of industrialization, exploration, or colonization was spearheaded by English speakers. While the Spanish and Portuguese started the spread of European languages in the fifteenth and sixteenth centuries, they were quickly overtaken by British colonization in the seventeenth and eighteenth centuries and the British-led Industrial Revolution in the eighteenth and nineteenth centuries. By the end of the nineteenth century and continuing through the twentieth century, American economic expansion further spread the need to speak, read, and understand English. This expansion continues today since the roots of digital and electronic commerce evolved in the English-speaking world.

This ongoing addition of words from other languages makes English quite possibly the most varied language in the world. We have many ways to express a single word. The prevalence of English, combined with the many synonyms resulting from taking other languages' words, offers the writer the opportunity to choose from many words to express ideas. Some of these words are simple, and some not so simple. It is tempting to choose the longer, more "educated-sounding" word, but your message is almost always better conveyed using the simpler, shorter word.

NOTE

1. *Source*: http://webspace.ship.edu/cgboer/evolenglish.html.

Chapter 2

How to Write in Plain English

For many people, their approach to writing consists of the following eleven steps:

1. Get the writing task.
2. Panic and moan.
3. Think about it for too long, so you are likely to miss your deadlines.
4. Panic and moan.
5. Start writing—don't have a plan and fill the document with jargon, acronyms, clichés, adjectives and adverbs, illogical sentences, big words, repetition, and massively lengthy and convoluted sentences and paragraphs.
6. Develop a case of writer's block.
7. Panic and moan.
8. Rush to get the darn thing done.
9. Kick it up to the boss or professor or editor and let them fix (rewrite) it.
10. Panic and moan.
11. Repeat steps 1 through 10.

But there is a better way . . . and here's the "secret."

The "secret" is simple: Understand and apply a logical process to everything you write. Make a habit of using this process, and writing becomes a straightforward task. The end result meets the needs and goals of your audience. Your documents become clear, concise, and usable. You are writing in plain English, using plain language. Your audience thinks you are wonderful because they can understand what you wrote and use the information you gave them.

So, how do you reach this pinnacle of simplicity and clarity? Apply these nine commonsense steps.

NINE STEPS TO ENSURE YOU ARE WRITING IN PLAIN ENGLISH

1. Identify and write to the "right" audience.
2. Keep it simple and short: Manage your words, sentences, paragraphs, and bullets.
3. Plan and organize your document before you start writing.
4. Apply the "Cs" and "Rs" of effective writing.
5. Use correct grammar and punctuation.
6. Use reader-friendly voice, tone, and person.
7. Apply effective self-editing and -proofreading techniques.
8. Write for the likely viewing medium.
9. Employ the principles of netiquette.

Sounds like a lot of work, doesn't it? Maybe at first, but as with most things, you will quickly see the benefits. Repetition will help you internalize the process, so it becomes instinctive, enabling you to create a quality-finished product in less time than you are currently spending.

Writing effectively and efficiently is much like painting a room. You could try to be really careful and hope you don't spill any paint, and maybe the room will look really great when you're done . . . or maybe not. Or you could take the time to apply the painting process: Take down blinds and rods; turn off breakers, remove light switch plates, and tape around the outlet edges; tape the baseboards and other seams; cover the carpet and furniture; and so forth. Then the painting goes really quickly and the room looks great . . . and with a bit of practice, the prep work takes less time and the end result comes increasingly quickly.

As with painting a room the "right" way, making writing a process and then applying that process takes time, but the end result is well worth the time spent.

So, let's get started and work through the process that makes writing in plain English a simple, straightforward process and ensures you will become a better, more confident writer.

Chapter 3

Identify and Write to the "Right" Audience

RULE NUMBER ONE: IT'S ALL ABOUT THE AUDIENCE—THE READER

> "A child of five could understand this. Send someone to fetch a child of five."
>
> —Groucho Marx

When we write, we have a tendency to write for ourselves and our reviewer or supervisor. This presents a problem. After the reviewer and supervisor have given their comments, from their perspective, you now have a document that may be very "audience unfriendly." If the intended reader doesn't see himself or herself in your document, one or more things may happen. The reader:

- May not read past the first paragraph or two
- May not understand what you are trying to convey
- May think he or she understands what you are trying to convey, but is mistaken
- May toss the document (or shut down the file) and do nothing
- May go to someone else for the answers or information or whatever

None of these actions is what you had in mind, but the reader doesn't know that. All he or she knows is you sent something they cannot read, understand, follow, or comply with. Documents that are clear, concise, and audience focused and audience friendly get read. They get favorable responses. Documents that are murky and writer focused are too often ignored or misunderstood.

IDENTIFY YOUR AUDIENCES

Who are your audiences? Every document is probably a bit different, and so may be the intended audience(s). It is very worthwhile to take a couple of minutes before you start the writing process and jot down your audiences. Audiences fall into several categories:

- Intended—the "actionees"
- Unintended—maybe the admin assistant, or someone in an "actionee's" office
- "Accidental—sending an email to John R. Smith when you meant John P. Smith"?
- Hostile—often a result of the dreaded "forward" action in response to an email
- Management chain—your managers, supervisors, reviewers who want the document written for them and then wonder why the desired responses are not forthcoming

Create a Purpose Statement

Once you have identified your intended and most likely unintended audiences, there is a second action you need to take. You need to create a simple, fifty-word purpose statement that describes the following:

- What you are going to write
- Who it is for
- What you want to happen as a result of the intended (and possibly unintended) audiences receiving your document

With these two pieces of information (audience and purpose statement) in hand, you will be better prepared to approach or email the management/review chain *before* you start writing and get their support and agreement for the document's focus.

WRITE TO THE LEVEL, NEEDS, AND GOALS OF YOUR MOST LIKELY AUDIENCES

The average high-school graduate usually reads at approximately a fifth- to sixth-grade level. If the material is in their area of expertise, they may read at a ninth- to tenth-grade level or a bit higher. The average college graduate usually reads at a ninth- to tenth-grade level, increasing to college level in their areas of expertise. Even a PhD usually only reads at a postgraduate level in his or her area of expertise. Give a PhD in antenna design and radio frequency propagation an excerpt from the doctoral thesis of a human behavioral specialist and the designer will throw up his or her hands in disgust and walk away.

Have you ever refused to read a newspaper or popular magazine because it was "too easy"? Probably not, and these forms of media are written at a high school level for the most part. What about a trade journal in an area outside your areas of interest or expertise? Journals or similar publications are generally written at a college level since the readers are expected to be very familiar with the general area.

When you are writing for the general public, unknown readers (such as those who visit a website), or people without your level of expertise, writing using simpler words and active voice will get better results and responses. If you want someone to do something, make your message and objectives as clear, concise, and complete as possible. Be considerate of the reader—their time, goals, needs, and level of expertise. As with the newspaper, most readers will appreciate clarity and simplicity.

Simple, considerate documents get more positive responses and better results . . . it's that easy.

We live in an age of too much information. Readers want to find or receive documents and information that only requires one reading to understand. In many instances, if someone has to read your material a second time, they simply won't do it, resulting in misunderstandings. People may read something a second time if it wasn't crystal clear the first time, but don't count on it . . . and they rarely read materials a third time.

Put yourself in your audiences' place. You wrote the material and probably don't want to reread it. You want them to learn or do something after reading your material. If you don't want to reread what you wrote, why would someone else? Write with the assumption you would be lucky if the reader goes through the document a second time, and, then, the reason for writing in plain language becomes very clear.

Chapter 4

Keep It Simple and Short

MANAGE YOUR WORDS, SENTENCES, PARAGRAPHS, AND BULLETS

"The greatest ideas are the simplest."

—William Golding, *Lord of the Flies*

Simplifying your writing is not the same as "dumbing down." Writing simply and concisely is a real challenge. Writing that is clear, concise, and to the point gets read. Writing that is text dense, jargon filled, laden with clichés, and designed to impress or overwhelm is often ignored or misunderstood.

Have you ever refused to read the newspaper because it was too "easy"? Do you seek out *The Economist* magazine or avoid it because it is "too hard"?

"People who pride themselves on their "complexity" and deride others for being "simplistic" should realize that the truth is often not very complicated."

—Thomas Sowell, *Barbarians Inside the Gates and Other Controversial Essays*

So, how do you write simply and clearly? Start by keeping in mind the "KISS" principle: Keep it short (or simple) and sweet.

In the previous step, we went through the need to focus on the audience when you write. Putting yourself in the intended audience's place can go a long way toward deciding how "simple" your writing needs to be. Applying some basic guidelines to your word choices, sentences, and paragraphs and using bullets form the backbone of simplification. You can (and should) still write the way you like to write, and then go back and apply the guidelines discussed in the next sections.

As you write and revise your writing or the writing of others, keep in mind the information given in table 4.1.

Table 4.1 Well-Written versus Poorly Written Documents: Results

Well-written documents—documents written in plain English—enable your readers to:	Poorly written, turgid, text-dense documents encourage your readers to:
Read what you write	Avoid reading what you write
Quickly understand what you write and what you are trying to accomplish—what you want from the reader	Misunderstand or misinterpret what you are trying to accomplish
Remember you, and your organization, favorably	Think about you, and your organization, unfavorably

MANAGE YOUR WORDS

Choose your words with care. Words such as "utilize" or "utilization" are intended to impress. Try "use" instead. The meaning is almost always the same, the sentence is simpler, and the focus is on the audience.

Review your writing with an eye to removing or replacing words and phrases. Words such as "that" and "which" are overused. They lead to other problems such as whether to use "who" or "whom." Minimize multiple adjectives, nouns, and adverbs: Use one rather than three or four.

Look out for hidden verb forms such as "managed the production of"—try "produced" instead (see table 4.2).

Table 4.2 Reducing Word Counts

Rather than:	Her ability to managerially focus her full, undivided, complete attention on the overly sensitive, pressing matters at hand enabled her to successfully make utilization of her vast, in-depth, comprehensive knowledge to evaluate complicated data and information and reach a reasoned, directly on-point solution. (*A 44-word sentence with a grade level of 26.5 and a reading ease of zero.*)
Try this instead:	She focused completely on the matters at hand. This enabled her to use her vast knowledge to assess complicated data and develop a suitable solution. (*Two sentences averaging 12.5 words with a reading ease of 48.6 and a grade level of 9.5.*)

The first example has "hidden" verbs (managerially focus), excessive adjectives, words designed to impress (utilization rather than use), a prepositional phrase (make utilization of), and far too many words for one sentence. The readability statistics show that it is considered "unreadable" and is written at a level well beyond postdoctoral.

The revised example eliminated "hidden" verbs by choosing one (focus). It has one adjective rather than two or three. The prepositional phrase and several multisyllabic words are gone.

Eliminating hidden verbs (also referred to as "nominalizations") is a very effective way to simplify your writing and self-edit at the same time. Table 4.3 provides a few more examples of hidden verbs and their amended versions.

Table 4.3 Hidden Verbs

Nominalized Form	Base Verb Form
We are responsible for the management of the program. (Reading ease: 40; grade level 9.6) • There is a verb—responsible—and a nominalized verb—management. • Adds length, not clarity or value	We managed the program. (Reading ease: 75.8; grade level: 3.6)
Our team conducted an analysis of the data. (Reading ease: 50.6; grade level: 8.) • The verb: conducted • The nominalization: analysis	Our team analyzed the data. (Reading ease: 66.4; grade level: 5.2)
Jody performed a reconnaissance of the proposed picnic site. (Reading ease: 47.3; grade level 8.8) • The verb: performed • The nominalization: reconnaissance	Jody previewed the proposed picnic site. (Reading ease: 59.7; grade level: 6.4) • In addition to avoiding the hidden verb, this sentence is much simpler since it doesn't have "reconnaissance" in it. • Reconnaissance is actually a form of jargon used mostly by the military and similar groups.

There is not an inherent problem with the examples in table 4.3, at least in terms of readability . . . but incorporating large numbers of these constructions will affect readability of the document as a whole. The process of removing nominalizations is a form of both self-editing and sentence simplification.

Avoid Jargon, Gobbledygook, and Clichés

Jargon and its siblings, gobbledygook and clichés, are everywhere. Long, complicated words and phrases may look impressive, but they are rarely reader friendly or audience focused.

Jargon is the specialized language of a professional, occupational, or other group; it is often meaningless or confusing to nonmembers. Gobbledygook is wordy, jargon-cluttered text that does not have a clear meaning. Clichés are trite phrases that have little or no meaning.

The world has become a very specialized place. Each profession, industry, institution, and so forth has a rich vocabulary of its own. Unfortunately, when you are writing for the general reader or the less specialized colleague, these unique terms put your writing into the realm of jargon and gobbledygook. When you start using jargon and gobbledygook, others may start to wonder about your level of knowledge. Your writing becomes convoluted, and your believability decreases.

How much is too much? It really comes down to two things: Who are the intended audiences and how familiar are they with your jargon? The broader the reach you want, the less jargon you should use.

When in doubt, write to the broadest possible audience—assuming the lowest level of understanding.

If you are writing to a nonnative English-speaking audience, they may have very limited understanding of most jargon, but a very deep knowledge of other jargon. In the academic world, nonnative speakers will understand highly specialized terms within their field of expertise. Outside of that environment, they may have very limited understanding of jargon (see table 4.4).

Table 4.4 Gobbledygook, Jargon, and Clichés

Gobbledygook	Bang for the buck: meaning to get the most (of something) for your money or effort. In the literal sense, this could mean other things, such as shooting at a male deer. This could be a problem for nonnative English speakers. In addition, "buck" is not synonymous with "dollar" in many cultures.
Jargon	*Any jelly bean with a pole can cork a meatball out of hard cheese. . . . In the distinctive jargon of what used to be called "our national pastime," any rookie (a "jelly bean") with a bat ("pole") can hit ("cork") a fastball ("hard cheese") that comes right down the middle of the plate (a "meatball").**
Cliché	Think outside the box.

The Dickson Baseball Dictionary, 3rd edition, by Paul Dickson (W.W. Norton & Co., 2009; paperback edition, 2011).

Consider the following example of gobbledygook and jargon.[1] The edited version is clear, simple, and readable; it follows the KISS principle (see table 4.5).

Table 4.5 Applying the KISS Principle

Before	After
After notification of NMFS, this final rule requires all CA/OR DGN vessel operators to have attended one Skipper Education Workshop after all workshops have been convened by NMFS in September 1997. CA/OR DGN vessel operators are required to attend Skipper Education Workshops at annual intervals thereafter, unless that requirement is waived by NMFS. NMFS will provide sufficient advance notice to vessel operators by mail prior to convening workshops.	After notification from NMFS, vessel operators must attend a skipper education workshop before commencing fishing each fishing season.

FIGURES OF SPEECH

"A figure of speech is a shifty thing; it can be twisted or it can be straight."

—Salman Rushdie, *Haroun and the Sea of Stories* (Granta, 1990).

Figures of speech can be very useful, or totally confusing. A figure of speech is the opposite of a literal expression: it is a word or phrase that means something more or something other than it seems to say.[2] Consider your audience and their level of knowledge. For example, if you are writing to a nonnative English-speaking audience, they will have very limited understanding of common English figures of speech (see table 4.6).

Table 4.6 A Figure of Speech: Example

"I'm quite sure he doesn't really think you have been abducted by aliens. It was just a **figure of speech**, like 'Oh, she's just little Miss Sunshine' or 'What a clown.' When you use expressions like that (which I totally never do), it doesn't mean a person is really an inhumanly hot solar ball or that they're a member of the circus. It's not literal."

Source: Laura Toffler-Corrie, *The Life and Opinions of Amy Finawitz*. Roaring Book Press, 2010.

When using figures of speech, you may be assuming a degree of sophistication or understanding that the audience does not have. You run the risk of being misunderstood and may even confuse or dismay your reader.

Some Common Figures of Speech

There are many so-called figures of speech. They serve a valuable purpose in different types of writing. However, when writing in plain English most figures of speech are best avoided. The potential for confusion or misinterpretation is too great.

Table 4.7 presents a short list. The ones in italics are explained; the rest can easily be found on the Internet.

Table 4.7 Summary: Figures of Speech

Non Sequiturs	Puns	Irony
Hyperbole	Analogy	Paradox
Overstatement	Allegory	Parody
Understatement	Simile	Satire
Superlatives	Euphemism	Sarcasm
Comparisons	Imagery	Word Play
Foreign Phrases and Expressions	Oxymoron	Fallacy

NON SEQUITURS

Many of the documents you write are used as aids in the decision-making process or are part of a report or other historical documentation. Non sequiturs pose a problem for those who must act upon or otherwise use your document. They simply don't make sense or don't apply to the situation. Overstatement, understatement, hyperbole, and superlatives are also out of place.

"A woman needs a man like a fish needs a bicycle."

—Irina Dunn

Humor, but not in professional or (most) other writing:

"If I had to live my life over, I'd live over a saloon."

—W. C. Fields

Example:

The police chief's reasoning was a non sequitur when he defended consulting a psychic "to help investigators crack the case" based on the premise that "we tried everything else and haven't solved the case." The fact that the case hadn't been solved using traditional police methods is irrelevant to whether consulting a psychic is a method that should be used. The error in reasoning should become obvious if we substitute "pick a name randomly out of the phone book to identify the main suspect" for "consult a psychic."[3]

HYPERBOLE/OVERSTATEMENT/UNDERSTATEMENT

"I'd rather be in prison in California than free anywhere else."

—Inez Haynes Irwin, *The Native Son*

Hyperbole is derived from a Greek word meaning "over-casting" and uses a figure of speech, which involves an exaggeration of ideas for the sake of emphasis (see table 4.8).

Table 4.8 *Hyperbole*: Example

"Everyone knows that."
"I can't do anything right."
"We examined every possible outcome/combination."
"It drives me nuts when employees are late."

Overstatement: Exaggerate; make a statement or claim that is not provable or reasonable or logical (see table 4.9).

> "The great enemy of the truth is very often not the lie, deliberate, contrived and dishonest, but the myth, persistent, persuasive and unrealistic."
>
> —John F. Kennedy

Table 4.9 *Overstatement*: Example

"The results of our analysis confirm there is absolutely no need for further exploration of the matter."

Source: Quote attributed (possibly incorrectly) to Charles H. Duell, the Commissioner of US patent office in 1899, "Everything that can be invented has been invented."

Understatement: A figure of speech is employed by writers or speakers to intentionally make a situation seem less important than it really is (see table 4.10).

> "When you hear that China is overcrowded, that's an understatement. I was shocked at the number of people. Even in the rural areas. I was also shocked at the poverty and at the living conditions."
>
> —Rosemary Mahoney

Table 4.10 *Understatement*: Example

"It rained a bit more than usual: while describing an area being flooded after heavy rainfall."
"Since the numbers we used are skewed, there is a slight possibility the results may not be valid."

SUPERLATIVES

"I responded in what I thought was the *most truthful*—or *least untruthful*—manner, by saying no."

—James R. Clapper, Director of National Intelligence, explaining why he told Congress in March 2013 that the National Security Agency doesn't intentionally collect data on millions of Americans.

Superlatives are a type of modifier. They add "most/least" to adverbs and adjectives or use -est. They are qualitative rather than quantitative. The prepositions "to" or "of" are normally used when making a comparison. One way to simplify your writing is to look for these superlatives and phrases with superlatives and comparisons and see if they are really necessary (see table 4.11).

Table 4.11 *Superlative*: Example

"She is the oldest of seven siblings." (Comparison; probably doesn't need to be deleted.)
"This is the strangest workplace." (Nothing to compare it to; probably should be explained or deleted.)

COMPARISONS

When making *comparisons* you normally use "-er" or "-est." Here's a simple way to know which ending is appropriate: If you are comparing two entities, use the two-letter "-er." If you are comparing three or more entities, use the three-letter "-est" (see table 4.12).

Table 4.12 *Comparisons*: Example

She has four siblings: two brothers and two sisters.
She is the eldest of the three girls.
She is older than the two other girls.
She is older than both of her brothers.
Richard is the older of the two brothers.

FOREIGN PHRASES AND EXPRESSIONS

Many *foreign phrases and expressions* have entered the English language and are clear to most people. Most of these phrases have everyday English equivalents, so it is usually best to use the plain English version.

How do you decide when or whether to use the foreign phrase? Consider your audience and how likely they are to really understand the phrase. Then ask yourself if you can use a simple English word or phrase instead.

For example, the meaning of the word "café" is clear to almost everyone. To substitute "restaurant" would not be logical or practical. On the other hand, to use the phrase "le dernier cri" might sound educated, but its meaning ("the latest thing") would be lost on most English-speaking audiences

USE SIMPLER WORDS

Simple words are usually unambiguous, but many simple words have multiple meanings. Nonetheless, if your sentences are written concisely and clearly and you use pronouns with care, there is little room to misunderstand your meaning. Rather than "utilize" consider "use," and rather than "utilization" try "usage" or "use" (see table 4.13).

Table 4.13 Word Simplification: Before/After

Before	After
Many noncollegially educated individuals, many of whom have never completed even a secondary level of education, routinely and consistently vote for funding for improving secondary and elementary schools.	Many residents, even those without a high-school diploma, regularly vote for better schools.

Table 4.14 presents some examples of complicated words and their simpler replacements:

Table 4.14 Word Simplification: Examples

Ameliorate	Make better, improve
Approximately	About, roughly, around, nearly
Bimonthly	Every two months
Component	Part, item
Demonstrate	Show
Enumerate	List, name
Fundamental	Basic
Necessitate	Require, need
Paradigm	Example, model
Prioritize	List, order, rank
Semiannually	Twice a year
Terminate	End

MINIMIZE INTRODUCTORY CLAUSES

In most cases, introductory clauses:

- Add unneeded length
- Degrade readability
- Weaken your case

There are exceptions, such as the introductory sentence in this chapter, where the clause makes sense. To see if you need to keep the clause, try the following:

1. Place it at the end of the sentence and make two sentences. Does it add anything? Should it still be at the beginning or can you delete it without impacting the meaning of your sentence or the point you are trying to make.
2. Try taking out a few words if the clause has more than two to three words.

Table 4.15 presents a few examples of introductory clauses that usually don't add value and do add words.

Table 4.15 Introductory Clauses: Examples

All things considered	Unless the exception in paragraph 2(b) applies
As a matter of fact	The point I intend to make is
In the event that	As a result of many meetings

AVOID PREPOSITIONAL PHRASES

Prepositional phrases are like introductory clauses, except they are often buried somewhere in the sentence. They almost always can be replaced by a single, simple word—often the preposition itself. See table 4.16 for a few examples.

Table 4.16 Prepositional Phrases: Examples

Prepositional Phrase	Change
Because of the fact that	Because
By means of	By
Make utilization of	Use
Have a tendency to	Tends (to)

MINIMIZE REDUNDANCY AND REPETITION

It's almost always better to write it once, and then move to your next point. The written (or electronic) word has a major advantage over the spoken one: Your reader can go back and revisit your words.

Repeating information can really annoy the reader. In addition, every time you repeat something you risk introducing an error or inconsistency or repeating one if it was there the first time.

The need for, and degree of, redundancy in a document is driven by document type and structure.

For example, if you are writing a journalistic piece, there is a set structure and word count that doesn't allow much repetition. The same applies to documents such as proposals since these are often page limited, making every word critical.

If you are writing a technical report or work plan, you may have to provide some amount of redundancy because of the required format. Many of these documents require an Introduction/Overview section, a Body with several sections, and a Conclusions or Recommendations section. In this case, there is some degree of repetition in each major section, in addition to the material in the Executive Summary. Nonetheless, this repetition should be minimized. The words and phrases should be virtually identical between sections to avoid introducing inconsistencies and errors.

SHORTEN YOUR SENTENCES

Once you've become more aware of the unneeded length and complexity of your sentences, and you've taken out extra words, jargon, phrases, and clauses, it's time to work on shortening your sentences.

Sentences should average ten to fifteen words. You can have sentences that are much shorter—sometimes a one- or two-word fragment is appropriate. You can have sentences that have twenty to thirty words. The key is balance, with an overall average (from readability) of fewer than fifteen words.

A variety of sentence lengths adds visual appeal to what you write. Your materials don't appear text dense. The shorter sentences and varied lengths make your document look readable even when it is fairly complicated.

Looks count. Documents that look easy to read almost always take precedence over those that look hard.

Consider table 4.17 for an example and the revised version with its shorter sentences.

Table 4.17 Sentence Simplification

Before	After
After carefully assessing the overall status of the program and the project status, and closely evaluating the projected outcomes against corporate goals, it was determined to expeditiously terminate the program and project. (Reading ease 5.1; grade level 20.)	We decided to quit. (Reading ease 76; grade level 2.6.)

SHORTEN YOUR PARAGRAPHS

Contrary to what Ms. or Mr. Smith taught in fourth grade, it is perfectly fine to have a single sentence paragraph. There are times when a single sentence paragraph is very powerful:

- To make or emphasize a point
- To transition between sections or ideas
- To make a document look less text dense

Just as with sentences, there are some basic guidelines for effective paragraph lengths. Again, these are not hard-and-fast rules, but they make very useful planning and structuring tools. Aim for two to six sentences in a paragraph. This approach solves the dilemma many people have—how to get out of a paragraph.

→ How do you get out of a paragraph? For most people the answer is simple: Type until you get bored or the paragraph looks too long, and then hit the ENTER key. Unfortunately, this approach does not generally lead to paragraphs with focus and clarity.

By limiting the average paragraph to two to six sentences of ten to fifteen words each, you manage three issues:

- You actively look for ways to shorten paragraphs, ensuring there is only one idea in a paragraph.
- You instinctively "see" where to break paragraphs to ensure there is no confusion in the reader's mind as to what you are addressing.
- You perform a type of self-editing since this formulaic approach often reveals other issues and errors.

Table 4.18 provides some simple ideas for managing paragraphs to make them more effective.

Table 4.18 Managing Paragraphs: Tips

Simple Guidance for Paragraphs
One idea = one paragraph
One idea can spread over several paragraphs
Related or subordinate ideas should get their own paragraphs
Two or more ideas ≠ one paragraph

By creating highly structured paragraphs, you can guide your reader through your document and ensure your meaning is absolutely clear.

Consider the example in table 4.19, and note how it lays out a framework for the text that would come next.

Table 4.19 Structuring Paragraphs: Example

In this section we are going to discuss four topics:
- Word choices
- Sentence structuring
- Paragraph management
- Using bullets

Now you can have four short paragraphs: one paragraph introduces each bulleted topic. You could use "soft" (bold or italicized) headings for each topic. You could also put all the information in one long paragraph, but then you run the risk of your audience not realizing where one topic ends and the next begins. You also risk interweaving the information in such a way that your meaning is not clear to the audience.

Having a mix of very short, short, and longer paragraphs makes your document look "easy"—more readable and audience focused. This approach also ensures your meaning is clear. Your document is visually appealing and more likely to be read and acted upon.

Consider this before and after example in table 4.20.[4]

Table 4.20 Paragraph Simplification: Before/After

Before	Scientific knowledge is not only uncertain, but also dynamic. Through research that is designed to reduce uncertainties, our understanding increases and, as a result, we change our assumptions about the impacts of environmental problems and how they should be addressed. For example, for many years we have been concerned mainly with removing large particles of toxic pollutants from airborne emissions, but recent research indicates that small particles of air pollutants may cause greater damage to human lungs than larger particles. This new information not only changes our understanding of the effects of air pollution, but also may significantly impact future pollution prevention and removal strategies. (Readability: ease = 26; grade level = 16)
After	Scientific knowledge is not only uncertain, but dynamic. Using research that is designed to reduce uncertainties, our understanding increases. This may change our assumptions about the impacts of environmental problems and how they should be addressed. For many years we have been concerned mainly with removing large particles of toxic pollutants from airborne emissions. Recent research indicates that small particles of air pollutants may cause greater damage to human lungs than larger particles. This new information not only changes our understanding of the effects of air pollution, but may also significantly impact future pollution prevention and removal strategies. (Readability: ease = 34; grade level = 12.5)

Source: http://www.epa.gov/osp/science.htm.

With a few simple changes, the "before" paragraph becomes more readable and the text looks "easier." Using the readability tool, you could make more changes to further improve the reading ease and reduce the grade level.

Use Bullets

Bullets are a very powerful tool for simplifying what you write. They also ensure your audience clearly "sees" the important points you are making.

Information you present also needs to be grammatically logical. Bullets go a long way toward ensuring your statements are logical, parallel, and properly punctuated. This is particularly true when you have "lists within lists," as the examples in table 4.21 show.

Table 4.21   Using Bullets to Ensure Paralel Sentence Structure

Before	Common sources of air leaks into a home include cracks around windows and doors, gaps along baseboard, mail chutes, cracks in brick, siding, stucco or foundation, or where any external lines (phone, cable, electric, and gas) enter the home.
Initial Bulleted List	Common sources of air leaks into a home include: • Cracks around windows and doors • Gaps along baseboard • Mail chutes • Cracks in brick, siding, stucco or foundations • Where any external lines (phone, cable, electric, and gas) enter the home
Revised Bulleted List	Common sources of air leaks into a home include: • Cracks around windows and doors • Gaps along baseboard*s* • Mail chutes • Cracks in brick *mortar*, siding, stucco or foundations • *Entry points for* external lines (phone, cable, electric, and gas)
After	Common sources of air leaks into a home include cracks around windows and doors; gaps along baseboards; mail chutes; cracks in brick *mortar*, siding, stucco, or foundations; and *entry points for* external lines (phone, cable, electric, and gas).

Source: http:/www.energy.gov (deleted from site).

Using bullets revealed several problems: the final bullet was not parallel with the first five; there are lists within lists, so each item needs to be separated by a semicolon, and there were likely missing words. As with shortening sentences and paragraphs, creating bulleted lists is another way to find errors and inconsistencies.

Table 4.22 explains the process when you are creating bullets. If you are going to keep the bulleted list, you only need to perform steps 1 and 2. If you are going to reassemble the items into a sentence, you follow all the four steps.

Table 4.22 Creating and Using Bullets: The Process

The Process: If you are presenting information that is essentially a list, and you don't want to use bullets, try the following to ensure your information is logical, parallel, and properly punctuated:

1. Make a bulleted list.
2. Revise as needed to ensure the list items are parallel.
3. Note where there are list items (in a single bullet) that require commas—because any sentence you (re)create is now going to need semicolons.
4. Reassemble the sentence.

USE SPELLING AND GRAMMAR CHECKING

Spelling and grammar checking are necessary evils. They are not infallible—in fact, they are often unreliable—but they are a good starting point. Since readability is linked to these checkers, it is really important to use the Spelling & Grammar tool.

A few notes:

- The grammar checker has issues with subject-verb agreement, so look at what it "suggests" very carefully.
- If you do not know the meaning of the word the spelling checker offers, look it up.
- The first choice the spelling checker offers may not be the correct one.

If you have seriously misspelled a word, the checkers will offer totally unrelated words in many cases. Another alternative is to use a "bad speller's dictionary." These are phonetically based and usually recognize the word you meant to use. There are several Web-based options such as the following:

- http://suggest.aspell.net/index.php/advance
- http://www.dumbtionary.com/

USE A THESAURUS

The thesaurus is your friend.

When you aren't sure of the meaning of a word, or how to spell a word, use the thesaurus. As long as you can come up with a synonym for the word you want, you can look up the synonym in the thesaurus. If your synonym is correct, the thesaurus will offer the word you want as an alternative. Even better, it will offer other words you may like better.

USE READABILITY

What is Readability and How does it Work?

Readability is a mathematically based scoring system that looks at many factors such as sentence length, number of syllables, and active/passive voice usage to determine the approximate "grade level" and "reading ease" of a passage or document. It is not infallible, especially when you are using bullets or creating acronyms. When selectively applied, it can be very useful for helping you simplify your writing.

One of the most commonly applied assessment tools is the *Flesch-Kincaid Reading Ease Calculator*. If you are using Microsoft Word, this calculator is an integral part of the spelling and grammar checking process. You do need to choose this feature; it is not part of the default settings.

To install the readability feature, see table 4.23.

Table 4.23 Installing Readability

→Go FILE (or the Windows button for some versions of Word).
→Click on FILE.
→Scroll down to the next-to-last item called OPTIONS.
→Click on OPTIONS. A new MENU (Word Options) will pop-up.
→Scroll down to the third choice called PROOFING.
→Click on PROOFING. A new MENU will pop-up.
→Look down this MENU for the check box to the left of SHOW READABILITY. Click this box.
→Click on OK.
Readability is now an integral part of spelling and grammar checking.

How does Readability Work?

It has two parts: the *Flesch* formula for reading ease—how "easy" it is for the "average" reader to comprehend something—and the *Kincaid* portion—what is the overall US grade level of the material (see table 4.24).

Table 4.24 The Readability Formula

The specific mathematical formula is:
$$RE = 206.835 - (1.015 \times ASL) - (84.6 \times ASW)$$

RE = Readability
ASL = Average sentence length (i.e., the number of words divided by the number of sentences)
ASW = Average number of syllables per word (i.e., the number of syllables divided by the number of words)

The output, that is, RE is a number ranging from 0 to 100. The higher the number, the easier the text is to read.

The Flesch Reading Ease Readability Formula[5]

Table 4.25 presents some general guidelines used when assessing the reading ease of your document.

Table 4.25 The Reading Ease Numbers: What They Mean

90–100: Very easy	50–59: Fairly difficult
80–89: Easy	30–49: Difficult
70–79: Fairly easy	0–29: Very confusing
60–69: Standard	

Source: http://www.readabilityformulas.com/flesch-reading-ease-readability-formula.php.

The average high-school graduate reads at about a fifth- to sixth-grade level. The ideal reading ease for that audience is should this be 60–100: somewhere in the standard to fairly easy range.

Applying Readability

Readability, when applied to an entire document, gives a good general sense of the level of complexity of the document. When combined with your knowledge of the intended audience, readability can be applied to the document several times, each time using the results to search for ways to simplify the document to make it more reader friendly.

In some cases, it's important to apply readability selectively because readability has several major shortcomings. These include how it handles the following:

- Creating acronyms
- Unavoidable long words
- Bulleted lists

Text with Acronyms

Acronyms are a necessary and unavoidable fact of most writing. Without them many documents would be entirely too long. But the long group of words the acronym replaces cause sentences to be unusually long, especially at the beginning of a document. This can give a skewed reading ease/grade level to the document, particularly if it is only a page or two in length. In cases where your document has lots of acronyms being created, it may be better to apply readability to portions of the document that aren't impacted by acronym creation.

To apply selectively in this situation, highlight the text you want to assess. Then, run *Spelling & Grammar* (under *Review*) on the highlighted text. When the pop-up box appears, asking if you want to check the remainder of the document, select *NO*. You will then get the dialog box showing the readability statistics for the section you selected (see table 4.26).

Table 4.26 Using Readability to Simplify Writing: A Tip

Tip→ Using readability scores to simplify your writing:

For the preceding two paragraphs the reading ease is 50.8 and the grade level is 10.3. Both are on the more difficult end of an acceptable score if this book were intended for a high-school audience. The primary cause of these scores is the length of the sentences. The average sentence has 16.7 words. There is only one passive sentence which does improve reading ease and reduce grade level.

If you were to try and improve the scores for these paragraphs, the starting point would be to try and break some of the longer sentences into two or more sentences. Then you would look for words to remove or replace with simpler words. Those two steps should easily improve the reading ease to 60–70 and drop the grade level to 9–10.

Unavoidably Long Words

Sometimes you have to use very long words because that is the correct or required terminology. If you have a paragraph or two with a lot of long words, you may want to leave it out of the readability calculation. But if you have multiple paragraphs with lots of difficult words, your document is going to be considered difficult to read. If at all possible, use the thesaurus to find alternatives unless you are certain your audience will understand what you wrote.

Bulleted Lists

In some cases, it's important to apply readability selectively. The formula has certain features that can cause bulleted lists to be interpreted as very long sentences—exactly what bullets are intended to avoid. Why does this happen? Because periods, explanation points, colons, and semicolons serve as sentence delimiters. If there are no delimiters, the readability tool apparently considers all the text as a long sentence that does not end until the next "delimiter." So, beginning with the colon that started the bulleted list, the readability doesn't think your sentence ends until it next encounters a period or other delimiter.

When applying readability in this situation, it is usually better to skip the bullets and highlight the text surrounding it. This means you have to run readability twice—once on the text preceding the bullets and once on the text following the bullets (see table 4.27).

Table 4.27 Applying Readability: Example

The Fair Credit Reporting Act (FCRA) requires each of the nationwide credit reporting companies—Equifax, Experian, and TransUnion—to provide you with a free copy of your credit report, at your request, once every 12 months. The FCRA promotes the accuracy and privacy of information in the files of the nation's credit reporting companies. The Federal Trade Commission (FTC), the nation's consumer protection agency, enforces the FCRA with respect to credit reporting companies.

A credit report includes information on where you live, how you pay your bills, and whether you've been sued or have filed for bankruptcy. Nationwide credit reporting companies sell the information in your report to creditors, insurers, employers, and other businesses that use it to evaluate your applications for credit, insurance, employment, or renting a home.

Here are the details about your rights under the FCRA, which established the free annual credit report program.*

Ease: 28.4
Grade: 15.3/13.8
Words/sentence: 24.6

First paragraph (where acronyms are being created:	Second and third paragraphs:
Reading ease: 28	Reading ease: 40
Grade level: 15.3	Grade level: 13.8
Words/sentence: ~24	Words/sentence: ~24

*http://www.consumer.ftc.gov/articles/0155-free-credit-reports.

"Any darn fool can make something complex; it takes a genius to make something simple."

—Pete Seeger

NOTES

1. http://www.plainlanguage.gov/examples/before_after/regfisheries.cfm.
2. http://grammar.about.com/od/fh/g/Figure-Of-Speech.htm.
3. http://www.skepdic.com/nonsequitur.html.
4. http://www.epa.gov/osp/science.htm.
5. http://www.readabilityformulas.com/flesch-reading-ease-readability-formula.php.

Chapter 5

Planning and Organizing Your Documents

"Simplicity is ultimately a matter of focus."

—Ann Voskamp, *One Thousand Gifts: A Dare to Live Fully Right Where You Are*

Remember in your fourth- or fifth-grade class when your teacher said something like, "Today we are going to learn about creating and using outlines to make your papers clear and logical." You've probably despised the idea of outlining ever since. Well, the outline is back, and is more useful than you may ever have imagined. It's a great way to get, and stay, focused on the writing task at hand.

The most effective (and efficient) way to create a logical, organized, readable document is to have a plan before you start and follow that plan through the entire writing process. The plan is simple: Create and use an outline.

CREATING AND USING OUTLINES AS DOCUMENT PLANNING TOOLS

Have you ever painted a room? Did you take the time to prepare the room first, or just try to carefully paint around everything and not get paint on the carpet, outlet plates, fixtures, and curtains? Preparation takes time—probably longer that actually painting the room—but with proper preparation, the actual painting goes quickly, and the end result is clean and attractive.

An outline is the key to ensuring you cover everything in your document that is needed—no more, and no less.

The process of creating an outline is straightforward:

- Make a list of the key points you need to cover.
- Prioritize these points.
- Integrate them with any template or standard format you need to follow.
- Coordinate with other people—team members, managers, subject matter experts, and so forth—to make sure you are covering all the "right" topics.
- Turn these key points into headings for sections.
- Apply a numbering (lettering) system to these key points.

Now, you have a framework with which to work: You have completed the initial prep work for your document.

You can write the document in almost any order you wish, keeping in mind that the Executive Summary should be written last. You can move headings around since you haven't complicated matters by writing text yet. You can ensure the headings and content for each topic are logical and parallel.

- When creating headings, each level 1 heading should be parallel, meaning they are of equal importance and start with the same word type—verb, or noun, and so forth. If you only have one heading at any level after level 1, you either need to create a second heading or not use a heading.

The two most common ways to capture the information for an outline are by using a table or a spreadsheet. If your outline, and the additional information you add, is simple, a table is usually sufficient. If you need to annotate with substantial information, consider using a spreadsheet. A very simple table could look like table 5.1.

Table 5.1 Sample Outline

Document Topics	Document Section	Author	Date Due	Management Sign-off
Executive Summary/Abstract				
Table of Contents	TOC List of Figures List of Tables			
Introduction				
Heading/Topic Key point Key point Key point	A A.1 A.2 A.3			
Heading/Topic Key point Key point	B B.1 B.2			

(Continued)

Table 5.1 *(Continued)*

Document Topics	Document Section	Author	Date Due	Management Sign-off
Heading/Topic	C			
Key point	C.1			
Key point	C.2			
Key point	C.3			
Key point	C.4			
Conclusions/Recommendations				
Appendices				
Appendix I	I			
Appendix II	II			
Bibliography/Citations				

Having this simple structure gives you great control over the writing process, as the next section explains.

USING OUTLINES TO MANAGE, ORGANIZE, AND WRITE YOUR DOCUMENT

Your outline is an excellent tool for managing and organizing documents. You can annotate it with additional information to help keep your writing project, and other participants, on track. Properly and fully annotated, the outline can be an excellent way to "manage the manager"—getting "buy-in" and management support before writing the document.

Most of the documents you write probably go through at least one or two levels of management approvals. In addition, these documents are often written by more than one person, adding several layers of difficulty and coordination to the writing task. Finally, you may also go through a formal editing and/or peer review cycle before your document is approved and released.

Taking advantage of a well-annotated outline allows you to manage these often conflicting and competing people and priorities. By providing a certain amount of administrative detail, you may be able to reassure sometimes difficult people that you have the writing process under control. You can also use this outline to manage the contributions from various writers and editors, reduce repetition and omissions, and overcome writer's block. And best of all, you can break sections into word, paragraph, and page counts to make everyone's writing roles as easy as possible.

How can this be? How does a simple outline do all this?

Table 5.2 expands on table 5.1 by taking a portion of the table and explaining its use in greater detail.

Table 5.2 Annotated Outline

Document Topics	Document Section	Author	Date Due	Management Sign-off
Executive Summary/Abstract →This section is always written last so it actually summarizes the document as it has been written. *Why?* How can you summarize something that does not yet exist? It's like summarizing a book for its jacket before the book is written. The reader starts reading and nothing aligns with the summary. Result? Confusion at best and big problems at worst.	→Add paragraph and word counts. Note this should be 5–10 percent of overall length, and no more than two pages.	→Note who is writing this section and who is reviewing it.	→A timeline with milestones and deadlines is very important.	→Make sure management sees the complete outline—keeping them involved makes "buy-in" and sign-off easier to obtain before writing.
Table of Contents	→This evolves from the first- (and possibly second/third-) level outline points.	→No specific author if automatic headings are used in document.		→Indicate who must sign off on this area.
Introduction	→Assign paragraphs based on 50-words/paragraph. Note there are about eight or nine 50-word paragraphs on a page of text.	→Note who is writing this section and who is reviewing it.	→A timeline with milestones and deadlines is very important.	→Indicate who must sign off on this area.
Heading/Topic *Key point* • Add additional points under each key point, making these third-level headings. Verify there are no redundancies unless document structure or directions require them. *Key point* *Key point*	→Assign paragraphs based on 50-words/paragraph	→Note who is writing this section and who is reviewing it.	→A timeline with milestones and deadlines is very important.	→Indicate who must sign off on this area.

The preceding activities need to be implemented and captured for each section of your document. By listing headings to the second or third level and adding a small amount of detail about each point, you accomplish three critical things: You ensure nothing is left out, reduce repetition to the bare minimum, and provide management with the reassurance you know what you are doing. You also provide quantitative guidelines to your authors so they know how much "space"—words and sentences and paragraphs—they have for writing their contribution.

You can put lots of other things in your outline. You might include review and coordination sessions, tips, references to be used, useful Web links, and anything else that makes your outline a useful planning, coordination, and management tool.

By having this level of detail, any author can write the assigned sections in any order, knowing the scope of the section and what goes in/does not go there. This is one of the best tools for overcoming writer's block since the document can be written in parallel rather than in serial format, and everyone knows what is expected.

→Tip: Providing page counts that specify sentence and paragraph length is very useful when you have multiple authors, authors who get easily overwhelmed, or page restrictions (as is often the case with proposals and articles for professional or other publications). Telling someone they need to address three main points, each with three subpoints, and each subpoint with three sub-subpoints, and telling them they have a total of one hundred fifty-word paragraphs to do so is far less daunting than telling them they must deliver twelve to thirteen pages of text. As soon as they "do the math," it becomes obvious they only have about four paragraphs per point (since the total of points, subpoints, and sub-subpoints is 27). They may even come back to you asking for more pages.

Chapter 6

Applying the "Cs" and Rs" of Effective Writing

"One should use common words to say uncommon things."

—Arthur Schopenhauer

What are the "Cs" and "Rs" of effective writing?

Table 6.1 lists the "Cs and Rs" of effective writing, followed by explanations and examples.

Table 6.1 The "Cs" and Rs" of Effective Writing

The "Cs"	The "Rs"
Clear	Readable
Concise	Reassuring
Correct	Rewarding
Complete	Responsive
Compliant	Responsible
Consistent	Requirements-driven
Considerate	

THE "Cs" OF EFFECTIVE WRITING

Clear Writing

Clear writing is something that can usually be understood by the intended reader the first time through. Writing that consistently requires a second or subsequent reading is not clear. Readers should not need to reread something, looking for shades of meaning, in order to understand your material.

Examples of clear and unclear writing are provided in table 6.2.

Table 6.2 Clear versus Unclear Writing: Examples

Clear Writing	Unclear Writing
Example 1	
The meeting will be at 3:00 p.m. Monday June 21, 2018, in room 217A. All members of Team B are required to attend.	The next meeting will be at the same time and place as two months ago but in the room on the third rather than second floor. Those listed in the previous agenda are required to attend along with all new personnel except from Team A.
Example 2	
The contract is to purchase three 15" 720 × 600 pixels monitors. These monitors are required to be delivered and installed by the vendor, not later than January 17, 2020. The maximum total cost for the monitors, installation, and one-year warranty is $4,000.00.	This is a contract to purchase up to $4,000.00 of quality monitors. They must be delivered and installed ASAP. The purchase prices should include all required components and services.

In *Clear Example 1*, it is very clear when the meeting will be held, where it will take place, and who should attend. In *Unclear Example 1*, the author has assumed a degree of knowledge that new employees may not have since they weren't here for the last meeting. It is also expected that prospective attendees know which teams are involved and which room on the second floor was the site of the last meeting so they can get to the correct room on the third floor. It is likely a number of key people will miss this meeting.

In *Clear Example 2*, the requirements of the contract, exact deliverables, required delivery and installation date, and total contract scope are quite clear. In *Unclear Example 2*, the contract is somewhat open-ended since no number of monitors or performance specifications are provided. The term "ASAP" (as soon as possible) is qualitative rather than quantitative, leaving the actual deliverables, dates, and so forth up to the contractor. In addition, it appears the contractor gets to decide what the required components and services are. The contracting officer or specialist is not going to be happy with the end result.

Concise Writing

Remember when you wrote papers in school? The teacher told you to write a ten-page paper on the history of the Nile and its impact on Egyptian civilization. After recovering from your initial panicking and moaning—ten pages? Is he crazy!?—you tried to devise ways to stretch your limited research and facts into ten pages. How did you do this? Probably, by writing in large letters or using a large-type font and adding more and longer words to each sentence.

Now, using longer words, additional words, and other techniques are too often embedded in the way we write, much to the detriment of our audience—the reader. One of the simplest ways to make your writing concise (and clear) is to look for certain types of words and phrases and eliminate or, at least, minimize them. Following are four of the easiest and most effective ways to make writing concise:

- Use one or two adverbs or adjectives rather than three, or four, or more for each verb or noun. Delete the others.
- Avoid, or minimize, the use of prepositional phrases. They add length and complicate the sentence, generally without adding value.
- Avoid, or minimize, the use of introductory and embedded clauses. In most cases, the clauses simply weaken your argument. If you really believe you need the clause (especially introductory clauses), move the clause to the end and make it a stand-alone sentence. You will probably decide you didn't need the clause after all.
- Look for lengthy, multisyllabic words, and use a thesaurus to find shorter, simpler ones.

Examples of each of the four preceding items with simpler alternatives are provided in tables 6.3.

Table 6.3 Simplification Before/After: Applying the Cs

	Before	After
Multiple adverbs/ adjectives	Ms. Jones is a truly exemplary and outstanding example and representation of the critical and key driving principles and standards of our organization and should be emulated by each and every employee.	Ms. Jones represents the highest principles of our company. She set an example for all employees to follow.
Prepositional phrases	We propose to make definitive utilization of our diverse and multifaceted corporation structure to achieve international standing and recognition as the best-in-class in our industry.	We will use our proven organizational structure to ensure we are the best-in-class in our industry.
Clauses	While in most cases the preferred approach to solving the problem is to work from data to solution, we propose to work from the solution backwards to specify the data sources needed for the project.	We propose to work from the solution backwards to specify the data sources needed for the project.
Lengthy words	Utilization Fraternize Information	Use Mix or mingle Data

→ Consider how writing military award recommendations often works. The perception is you need at least two adjectives for each noun for an Achievement Medal, three adjectives for a Commendation Medal, and four or more for higher-level awards. Much the same can probably be said for government (federal, state, and local) and corporate or association awards.

Correct Writing

Correct writing has been "sanity-checked": This means spell- and grammar-checked, assessed for readability, validated for correct use of words, cross-checked, united into a single voice and tone, and edited and proofread.

Keep in mind that it is very helpful to have someone else, even if he or she is not a "professional editor," review your document for the preceding items. If you write something, and there is an error, you will like it even better the next time you read it. Unfortunately, if there is something wrong, it will still be wrong, and you probably still won't notice the problem. Chapter 9 discusses some ways to self-edit when there is no editor or colleague available to help with sanity checking.

Complete Writing

Complete writing is like an invitation. You expect to provide everything the reader needs to do what you need, reach a conclusion, make a recommendation, or reach some other outcome. In other words, your writing needs to provide an "invitation" to the reader by including who, what, when, where, why, how, and how much.

If you want someone to provide you input for a report, your communications with that person need to be complete. This can be done by asking them the following questions:

- Who is involved in providing input (that person and others) and for whom is the report being prepared?
- What is the report covering, what are the milestones, and what is expected from your colleague(s)?
- When are the inputs due, when are the meetings scheduled, and when are the report milestones and final document due?
- Where are the inputs to be provided and where are the meetings to be held?
- Why are they being asked to participate and why is the report necessary?
- How to reach you and other team members, how to prepare their inputs, and how to get assistance with issues?
- How much time there is for them to prepare their inputs and how much material (pages, word counts, etc.) you expect from them?

Providing this level of detail, often in the form of an annotated outline (Step 4), forms the basis for a management coordination and sign-off tool, reducing misunderstandings and ensuring the end result is complete and reader friendly.

Compliant Writing

Compliant documents follow all guidelines and regulations. For example, if you are supposed to integrate company style guidelines and a standard style guide such as the *Chicago Manual of Style*, your document actually does this. If you are supposed to use an older version of MS Word, or use Open Office, your document does this. If you are supposed to adhere to strict page or word counts, fonts and font sizes, margins, and so forth, your document does this.

Compliance can be particularly critical for regulatory writing and for proposal writing. In both cases, there are generally very strict, published guidelines for length, font, word choices, tone, voice, person, structure, and more. Failing to follow any requirement, no matter how seemingly trivial, may be grounds for rejection of your document. In the case of a proposal, this rejection may be final, resulting in the waste of many hours of uncompensated work. In the case of regulations or similar documents, noncompliance may result in major revisions and delays.

Examples of noncompliance include the following:

1. Not writing in plain language when preparing a prospectus or similar document in the financial services area
2. Using Office 2010 when the request for proposal (RFP) clearly stated to use Office 2007
3. Using 11-point Garamond when the source document required 12-point Times New Roman—it did not indicate "12-point Times New Roman or equivalent"
4. Deliberately leaving out required information, enclosures, or other information

Consistent Writing

"Consistency" in your writing is really just another term for avoiding surprising or confusing the reader. Style guides go a long way toward assuring consistency, but many organizations have limited guidelines at best. In the absence of specific guidelines (either from your organization or from the intended reader's organization), there are two initial steps you can take.

First, ensure whatever you write is by using consistent fonts, formats, and structure throughout. Keep the voice, tone, and person consistent (see chapter 8 for examples). Avoid using more than two different fonts—one for the text, tables, and figures and one for the headings.

Second, in the absence of any other guidelines, especially for proposals, résumés, cover letters, and other solicitation-type documents, mirror the formats used by the supplier of the source document (the RFP, job advertisement, or similar document).

Minimize or avoid the use of all capital letters, bold or italic words (unless it is a title), ampersands (&) (unless part of a name or title), excessive punctuation (few or no "!" or "?"), underlining, changes of font type or size, colored fonts, jargon and slang, social media shorthand (RU, 4, LOL, etc.), and emoticons.

If your signature area in emails has a tagline or saying or biblical verse or quote, please delete it. Recipients may not see these things the same way you do.

There is always the possibility your document, and covering email message, gets forwarded to someone else and they don't appreciate your quote or use of emphasis, and your document is less-than-favorably received as a result.

Considerate Writing

Considerate documents are always audience- and reader focused. It is essential to keep in mind the needs and goals of your likely readers and write accordingly. Documents written for you (and your management) may work internally, but once the material is sent to the client, submitted in a proposal or report, placed on your website, and so forth, it must work for the reader.

Considerate writing uses tools like readability (see chapter 2) and estimates the most effective reading ease to make the document reader friendly. It uses plain language, applying the preceding five "Cs" of effective writing.

Is this considerate?

> Enter (I hope) the long sentence: the collection of clauses that is so many-chambered and lavish and abundant in tones and suggestions, that has so much room for near-contradiction and ambiguity and those places in memory or imagination that can't be simplified, or put into easy words, that it allows the reader to keep many things in her head and heart at the same time, and to descend, as by a spiral staircase, deeper into herself and those things that won't be squeezed into an either/or.[1]
>
> An 87-word sentence . . . perfectly correct, but grade level is 35.7 and reading ease is "zero."

THE "Rs" OF EFFECTIVE WRITING

As with the "Cs" of effective writing, there is another set of adjectives that describe audience-friendly writing—the "Rs" of effective writing.

Readable Writing

Knowing the intended audience for a document is essential to ensuring that the document is actually read by that audience. It is very helpful to set standards for the document once you have created your purpose statement and identified the intended and most likely audiences. If you know you are writing to a general audience, the grade level should be fairly low—perhaps fifth-sixth grade—and the reading ease fairly high—around 60–70. Sentences should be short (ten to twelve words on average) and paragraphs equally brief (two to four sentences on average).

For more knowledgeable audiences, or industry-specific groups, the grade level, reading ease, sentence length, and paragraph length can be more difficult, but remember, people rarely get upset over "easy" reading.

No matter what your audience's interest or reading ability is, writing in active voice is almost always the best choice. This way the reader "sees" himself or herself in the document and realizes something is needed on his or her part.

Table 6.4 gives an example of a short document that has been written in three ways—one for a general audience, one for a group of college science students, and one for a seminar of industry specialists or graduate meteorology students.

Reassuring Writing

Readers want to know that you understand what they need. They also want to be sure they understand what you want, need, or expect from them. Writing that is clear and concise conveys your message and reassures the reader that what you want is attainable and understood.

Rewarding Writing

Effective writing is a win-win-win. You win. The readers win. Your manager or other responsible individual wins. It doesn't get much better than that.

Rewarding writing is writing that gets results—the results or responses you want, in the format you want, by the time you require, with little or no clarification needed.

Consider the case of a résumé. A "rewarding" résumé leaves the reader with no doubt you are the right person for the opportunity. The reviewer or

Table 6.4 Sample Document: Three Audience Levels

General Audience	College Science Students	Industry Specialists or Graduate Meteorology Students
The Topic: Strong El Niño Expected in 2016 and Beyond*		
Our weather is being impacted by a very strong El Niño. During 2015, sea temperatures in the Pacific Ocean were higher than normal. The air moving above the Pacific and Indian Oceans is affecting our weather very strongly. The result is many areas of the USA will have more rain and snow than usual.	A strong El Niño continued during November as indicated by well above-average sea surface temperatures (SSTs). Key indices rose to their highest levels so far. Subsurface temperatures in the eastern Pacific decreased slightly, but are still well above average. The traditional and equatorial Southern Oscillation Index (SOI) values remained negative. These conditions are associated with enhanced convection over the central tropical Pacific and suppressed convection over Indonesia. The net result is a very strong El Niño.	A strong El Niño continued during November as indicated by well above-average sea surface temperatures (SSTs) across the central and eastern equatorial Pacific Ocean (Figure 1). The Niño-4, Niño-3.4 and Niño-3 indices rose to their highest levels so far during this event, while the Niño-1+2 index remained approximately steady (Figure 2). The subsurface temperatures in the central and eastern Pacific, while still well above average, decreased slightly (Figure 3) due to the eastward push of the upwelling phase of an equatorial oceanic Kelvin wave (Figure 4). Low-level westerly wind anomalies and upper-level easterly wind anomalies continued over the most of the tropical Pacific. The traditional and equatorial Southern Oscillation Index (SOI) values remained negative. These conditions are associated with enhanced convection over the central tropical Pacific and suppressed convection over Indonesia (Figure 5). Collectively, these atmospheric and oceanic anomalies reflect a strong El Niño episode that has matured.
Readability and Other Statistics		
Grade level: 8.9 Reading ease: 55.2 Passive sentences: 25% Words/sentence: 13.5 # Paragraphs: three with 1.33 sentences.	Grade level: 12.7 Reading ease: 25.8 Passive sentences: 0 Words/sentence: 12.6 # Paragraphs: five with 1.5 sentences each.	Grade level: 15.9 Reading ease: 18.8 Passive sentences: 0 Words/sentence: 21.2 # Paragraphs: one with seven sentences.

*http://www.cpc.ncep.noaa.gov/products/analysis_monitoring/enso_advisory/ensodisc.html.

hiring manager can see exactly how you will help the company or the team meet key goals and deliver projects on time and budget.

Responsive Writing

This is writing that answers the asked and implied questions and meets the stated and unstated requirements. It is also timely, considerate, and complete.

Consider the case of a proposal. To be responsive, a proposal must do many things. It must follow all the directions. It must be 100 percent compliant. It must be easy to follow since it should be logical, organized, and written in clear, plain English. It must arrive on time. The solutions offered must align with the requirements in the solicitation documents.

Responsible Writing

It is essential to deliver complete, accurate documents in the required timeframe. These documents must be thoroughly researched or vetted, and properly referenced with complete citations and full credit given to sources.

Requirements-Driven Writing

It is tempting to offer more than what is being sought, but better to follow directions, request clarifications, and don't do things that might indicate a customer or other entity doesn't know what it wants. This is not a case where it is better to "ask forgiveness later rather than ask for permission now."

Adding what is often called "fluff," and sometimes known as "spin," is not generally a way to demonstrate that you are requirements-driven.

NOTE

1. *Source*: http://articles.latimes.com/2012/jan/08/entertainment/la-ca-pico-iyer-20120108.

Chapter 7

Using Correct Grammar and Punctuation

Good, clear grammar and punctuation are absolutely essential to ensure your reader—your audience—understands what you wrote, what your goals are, and what they are to do next. Grammar has many components and constructions; punctuation takes many forms. Table 7.1 lists the most commonly used and misused forms and components.

Table 7.1 Common Grammar and Punctuation Components

Grammar	*Punctuation*
Misplaced modifiers	Commas
Unclear sentences	Semicolons
Passive voice	Colons
Comma splices and comma splices	Quotation marks
Subject-verb agreement	Apostrophes
Incorrect pronouns	Exclamation points and question marks
	Bullets
Other	
Acronyms	Highlighting: Bold, Italics, and Underlining

GRAMMAR

Misplaced Modifiers

A modifier is a word or phrase that tells the reader a bit more about something. It is added to the sentence. The key is to add the modifier in the correct place—so it modifies, or gives more information about, the correct entity. Since there is a tendency to add modifiers after the sentence has been written, modifiers tend to end up at the end of the sentence rather than where they belong. Sometimes the result is funny, but other times it can be confusing or even problematic.

Consider the examples given in table 7.2.

Table 7.2 Misplaced Modifiers: Examples

Example	Comments
Cell phone video from the Sunday incident shows the woman, who has not been identified, crying as a crew member asks her to exit the aircraft repeatedly.*	Is the crew member asking the woman to exit the plane, reenter, and exit again, and then repeat the process? Or, is she being asked over and over again to get out—and she isn't moving?
I saw a statue of the famous playwright walking down Oak Street.	Really? A statue out for a stroll? Interesting sight. Perhaps the writer meant this: While walking down Oak Street, I saw a statue of the famous playwright.
This directive applies to Alaskan migratory birds set to expire on April 30, 2020.	Really? All the migratory birds in Alaska are scheduled to die on April 30, 2020? Or is it the directive that expires?
At ten years old, her mother gave her a new bicycle.	Really? The girl's mother was only ten, already had a child, and gave that child a bicycle? The modifier, "At ten years old," needs to go next to or immediately following the child, not the mother. "Her mother gave her a bicycle when she was ten years old."

*http://news.yahoo.com/woman-gets-booted-off-flight-prompting-fellow-passengers-154004296--abc-news-topstories.html.

As soon as you feel you need to add something to a sentence, look very carefully at where you put it. First, ask if the additional words are really necessary. Then read the sentence carefully to make sure the modifier is really modifying the right entity. The modifier needs to be placed as close as possible to what it is modifying. Ideally, the modifier should precede what it is modifying. If this is not logical, the modifier must be immediately following the modified entity.

Unclear Sentences

You know what you mean, but your written words may not have the same meaning to your readers. Simple sentences leave little room for misinterpretation. You maintain control of your message and have more influence on how the reader construes your meaning. You also avoid the temptation to "spin" your meaning into something less serious or something more favorable.

Choosing the right word—the correct meaning—is essential, too. Consider the following examples paraphrased from actual letters written to welfare or Medicaid offices:

- I am forwarding my marriage certificate and birth certificates and five children, one of which is mistaken as anyone can tell.
- I am very discouraged to find you have branded my twins illiterate. This is a rotten lie as I was married a week before they was born.

Passive Voice

Passive voice is very useful in some situations, but not when your goal is to write clearly, concisely, and in an audience-friendly style. Active voice is directive and takes ownership; passive voice avoids directives that are specific to any particular reader or audience. Legal documents are often written in passive voice, as are regulatory documents.

→Tip: Passive voice can sound "accusatory," especially when writing rules, guidelines, and regulations. If you are imposing a requirement, such as rules for employee parking, it is usually better to say, "These rules must be followed by all employees," rather than, "You must follow these rules."

If you want you reader to do something or understand something applies to him or her, active voice is almost always the best choice. If the objective is informational, passive voice may be fine.

→Tip: In active voice, the subject is doing or taking the action. In passive voice, the doer of the action is de-emphasized (see table 7.3).

Table 7.3 **Passive Voice: Examples**

Sample Sentence	Comments/Corrections
You will be responsible for validating the metadata associated with paper versions of library material (books, movies, music, etc.). Data such as title, description, author, and category will be reviewed and cleaned up.	Note the switch from active voice (first sentence) to passive voice (second sentence). The implication is that the review and clean-up will be done by some unspecified entity. Change the second sentence to: The data analysis team will review and clean up the description, author, category, and other data.
The employee kitchen must be cleaned at the end of the day.	You must clean the kitchen at the end of the day when your name appears on the roster.

If you are not sure if something is in passive voice, use the spell- and grammar checker to review the sentence(s) in question. The statistics will indicate the percentage of passive sentences—but the checker is not 100 percent reliable. A simple, but not infallible, way to look for passive voice is to look for forms of "to be" and "to have." Then look for the "actionee" or activity—if it is at the end of the sentence, the sentence is likely passive, and the "fix" is to move the "actionee" or activity to the beginning of sentence so you can change the verb to an action one. Table 7.4 gives some examples of passive active voice changes.

Table 7.4 Passive to Active Voice: Before/After

Passive Voice (Before)	Active Voice (After)
It was decided to quit.	We decided to quit.
Presidents are elected every fourth year.	We elect our president every four years.
Turn signals must be used.	You must use your turn signal.
Great musical performances are intended to be very moving for audiences.	We want our performance to move you.
Instead of this . . .	*Try this . . .*
It is recommended that . . .	We recommend . . .
The "as-built" diagram is the way the building should be remodeled.	Use the "as-built" diagram for all phases of remodeling.
It is important to . . .	You must . . .

Comma Splices and Run-on Sentences

A comma splice results when you use a comma—rather than another word or form of punctuation—to join what should be two sentences. A run-on sentence is two sentences joined without even the benefit of a comma.

Avoiding these two closely related grammatical errors is simple.

You can do it the easy way. Look for ways to shorten your sentences, and the problem will almost always resolve itself into two sentences.

You can do it the somewhat more complicated way. Manage the sentence in one of several ways:

- Use a semicolon to join the two sentences or eliminate the run-on.
- Use a coordinating conjunction to tie the two parts into one sentence.
- Use a subordinating conjunction to show the relationship between the two parts.
- Use a semicolon and transitional word followed by a comma.

These are the formats that make the most sense in many professional settings.

Table 7.5 gives examples of all five approaches to resolving comma splices and run-on sentences.

Table 7.5 Resolving Comma Splices and Run-On Sentences

Original Sentence with Comma Splice: Martha is a great team player, she always gets her reports completed on time.
Original Sentence as a Run-on Sentence: Martha is a great team player she always gets her reports completed on time.

Two sentences	Martha is a great team player. She always gets her reports completed on time.
Semicolon	Martha is a great team player; she always gets her reports completed on time.
Coordinating conjunction (and, but, for, yet, nor, so)	Martha is a great team player so she always gets her reports completed on time.
Subordinating conjunction (after, although, before, unless, as, because, even though, if, since, until, when, while)	Martha is a great team player because she always gets her reports completed on time.
Semicolon and transitional word (however, moreover, on the other hand, nevertheless, instead, also, therefore, consequently, otherwise, as a result)	Martha is a great team player; moreover, she always gets her reports completed on time.

Subject-Verb Agreement

Spell- and grammar checkers do a so-so job of identifying areas where the subject and verb do not agree. However, sometimes the checkers get very confused and offer options that make no sense. This is one of those areas where you need to carefully review your document. A major problem for many people is those odd words—data/datum, media/medium, and so forth—where the plural "sounds" singular. Other problems arise when the verb and subject are widely separated (usually because you used lots of adjectives, adverbs, and lists in your sentence).

The terms "data" and "media are particularly confusing for many writers and their readers. In most cases, these terms are plural. However, if you aren't comfortable with making the associated verb plural, there are two alternatives to consider:

- Add the word "set" before or after data: The set of data is clearly marked in the report. "Set" is a collective word in this case, so it is singular. If you place it after "data," the effect is the same: The data set is clearly marked in the report.
- Use an alternate word such as "information": The information is clearly marked in the report. In American English, "information" is always singular.

While using the grammar checker, look at each area that it flags for subject-verb agreement. This will help you understand what the disagreement is and how to fix it. But remember the checker is not always right.

Table 7.6 presents some examples of disagreeing subjects and verbs, paired with their corrections.

Table 7.6   Resolving Subject-Verb Disagreements

Subject-Verb in Disagreement	Subject-Verb in Agreement
The data is clear.	The data are clear.
My preferred paper media is the magazine.	My preferred paper medium is the magazine.
I'm working to ensure the services the NSA and NIST provides can be applied as an effective public tool.	I'm working to ensure the services "they" provide can be applied as an effective public tool.

Note that in the last example in the preceding table, the paired acronyms "NSA and NIST" were replaced by "they." This replacement technique is a simple way to ensure you are using plural verbs where appropriate. When you have decided on plural versus singular, you can put the acronyms back.

Incorrect Pronouns

There are many ways to use pronouns incorrectly. We will go through two of them in this section.

First, there is using pronouns that do not match the plurality of the noun to which they refer. This goes directly to the classic dilemma of how to avoid using him/her. While replacing the paired him/her or himself/herself with they or their or them is commonly used, it is not really correct. By changing to second person (you) or reformatting the pronoun, the problem can be avoided altogether.

Consider the example given in table 7.7.

Table 7.7   Pronoun Use: Examples

Incorrect Pronoun Use	Correct Pronoun Use
Everyone must drive their own car.	Everyone must drive his or her own car.
Avoidance alternative #1 (second person):	You must drive your own car.
Avoidance alternative #2 (third person):	Attendees must drive their own cars.

→Tip: The process of working around this grammatical issue helps you find other problems and errors. Avoidance and rewriting are excellent self-editing and simplification tools.

Second, there is the dilemma of when to use "which, that, who, or whom" and when to use he versus him, she versus her, and us versus them.

In American English, if "that" makes sense, we almost always use "that" rather than "which" (see table 7.8).

Table 7.8 Which versus That

Using "Which"	Using "That"
Correct: Which way are you going?	Incorrect: That way are you going?
Incorrect: This is the car which I want to drive.	Correct: This is car that I want to drive.

We also have a tendency to use "that" when referring to people. People are "who" or "whom" or "him or "her," and so forth. When you are using "that" or "which," and referring to people, try replacing the word with "who." Now you have your nouns and pronouns almost properly aligned . . . but, should you be using "whom" rather than "who"? Here is a simple test:

1. See if you can replace "which" or "that" with "who" while keeping the meaning of the sentence intact and aligning the nouns and pronouns (e.g., people with who/whom and animals/things with that/it).
2. Revise the sentence to put the "who" or "whom" after any preposition.
3. If the sentence still makes sense (albeit soundly a bit archaic), you should be using "whom." Otherwise, you need to use "who."
4. Now revise the sentence to use the correct pronoun you have identified.
5. Finally, question whether you needed the pronoun (or that/which) in the first place.

The process flows as shown here:

- Look for the pronoun or its stand-in (that/which): This is the person which I was telling you about.
- See if you can replace "which" with "that" and not impact the meaning: This is the person that I was telling you about.
- Now replace "that" with "who": This is the person who I was telling you about.
- Next, revise the sentence to place the pronoun "who" after the preposition "about": This is the person about who I was telling you.
- The sentence still makes sense, although it sounds archaic, so that means you need to use "whom" rather than "who."
- The correct form would be either "This is the person whom I was telling you about." or "This is the person about whom I was telling you."
- Keeping in mind the fact that "that" (and which) are vastly overused, try going back to the first two steps and take out "that" or "which." You didn't even need the word in the first place: This is the person I was telling you about.

Another example of how simplification—in this case deleting one simple word—can solve a lot of grammatical issues and problems.

Another way to solve the pronoun dilemmas is to substitute "him" or "her" when you are not sure if you should use "whom" or "who": replace the pronoun with "him" or "her." If this replacement sounds "less bad" than using "he" or "she," you almost always want "whom" rather than "who."

Using the "pronoun following preposition" technique is a very effective way to ensure you are using the correct pronoun. There are 70 commonly used prepositions,[1] and about 150 in total; and countless prepositional phrases moving pronouns around to perform this simple check is a great way to self-edit and eliminate unneeded prepositional phrases and hidden verbs at the same time.

Table 7.9 shows the common pronouns. If you can place a pronoun from column "B" after a preposition and the sentence still retains the correct meaning, then the pronoun needs to come from column "B." If it doesn't work, use the version from column "A."

Table 7.9 Common Pronouns

Column A	Column B
I	Me
You	You
He/She/It	Him/Her/It
We	Us
They	Them
Who	Whom

PUNCTUATION

Commas

Commas matter. There is a tendency to put a comma where you might pause when speaking. These commas are unnecessary and may change your meaning or otherwise confuse your reader see table 7.10.

Table 7.10 Comma Placement: Before/After

Sample and Corrected Version	Comments
Sample: Let's eat Grandma!	Do you really mean to eat your grandmother? Needs a comma!
Corrected version: Let's eat, Grandma!	Now you are telling your grandmother you are ready for dinner. She is no longer the main course!
Alternative: Grandma, let's eat!	

Commas are used to separate lists of "like" things: all nouns, all verbs, all adjectives, and so forth. Misplacing or adding a comma can totally change your meaning. The use of a comma where it doesn't belong forms the title of a very useful book called *Eats, Shoots & Leaves: The Zero Tolerance Approach to Punctuation* by Lynn Truss.[2] By adding a comma after the verb "eats," the entire list was turned into verbs rather than one verb and two nouns . . . and a panda became an armed marsupial. The sentence should have been: "Eats Shoots and Leaves."

Within lists there are often other lists. This brings up another punctuation dilemma: How do you know where to put commas when there are lists within lists? If you go back to the section on using bullets, you will see there were several examples of situations where commas weren't quite enough. If you have lists within lists, you must either separate the first-level lists from one another using semicolons or create bulleted lists. In professional writing, bulleted lists are almost always the simpler, cleaner solution.

Commas are used to set off introductory or lead-in clauses. Sometimes you need these clauses; at other times you can either eliminate them or move them to the end of the sentence and make two sentences. Commas are also used to distinguish clauses inside your sentences. Table 7.11 presents an example of these clauses.

Table 7.11 Introductory and Internal Clauses: Examples

Introductory Clause	*Internal Clause*
Except as stated in paragraph 3.b., all submissions must contain the complete property description, lot number, and filing date.	We are planning to go to lunch at The Fort, but Joe, a really annoying guy from Team B, insists on tagging along.
Revised sentence with explanation: All submissions must contain the complete property description, lot number, and filing date. The only exception is explained in paragraph 3.b. →Note that by putting the exception first, you are tempting people to assume they fall under the exception so they can avoid assembling all the information required. It is much better to make the introductory clause the second sentence, and then decide if it even needs to be included or if it is just weakening your case or argument.	Revised sentence with explanation: We are planning to go to lunch at The Fort. It appears Joe from Team B wants to come as well. →The internal clause is really an "aside" or modifier. It is probably not the kind of thing you would want to send in an email that might end up in Joe's inbox. It adds nothing to the statement and is better left out. Even as revised, it might be best to leave the second half off. Remember email never dies and can take on a life of its own.

Placement of commas is essential to conveying your intended meaning. The example from the Truss[3] book shows what happens when you use a comma incorrectly to separate "unlike" items. But there are some other times when comma placement can drastically alter your meaning. Consider this example:

"I would like to thank my parents, Lady Gaga and Einstein, for my success."

Really? Very interesting parents! This is a case where the comma before "and" is absolutely essential. Otherwise, you are creating a clause, or aside, that makes for a very interesting set of parents. The comma after Einstein is also incorrect.

A note about commas before "and": Both the *AP Stylebook* and the *Chicago Manual of Style* now specify the serial, or Oxford, comma. That means you need to use a comma before "and" in a list of "like" things, unless doing so changes the meaning.

Semicolons

Semicolons are a great way to hang on to your long sentences while applying the KISS principle. A semicolon is like a period, but not quite as definitive. From a readability perspective it is treated like a period, but from a writer's perspective it is like getting to hang on to long sentences. A win-win situation.

When should you use a semicolon?

Table 7.12 gives examples of when to use a semicolon.

Table 7.12 Using Semicolons: Examples

When to Use Semicolons	
Joining what is otherwise two sentences:	Joined with a semicolon:
The normal time for the meeting is 10:00 a.m. on Tuesdays. This week the meeting will be at 9:00 a.m. on Monday.	The normal time for the meeting is 10:00 a.m. on Tuesdays; this week the meeting will be at 9:00 a.m. on Monday.
Breaking up two sentences that have been joined with a conjunction or similar construction:	Joined with a semicolon:
The normal time for the meeting is 10:00 a.m. on Tuesdays but this week the meeting will be at 9:00 a.m. on Monday.	The normal time for the meeting is 10:00 a.m. on Tuesdays; this week the meeting will be at 9:00 a.m. on Monday.
Separating multiple item lists without using semicolons:	Separated with semicolons:
Our favorite color combinations are: pink and peach, red, blue, and green, yellow, green, and white, and purple, orange, black, and rose.	Our favorite color combinations are: pink and peach; red, blue, and green; yellow, green, and white; and purple, orange, black, and rose.
→Note that this sentence is very confusing if semicolons are not used.	→Note that a bulleted list might be even more effective and the punctuation is much simpler.
→Note that colon to introduce the list is not absolutely necessary.	→Note that a colon to introduce the bulleted list is necessary.
	→Note that the semicolon before "and" is necessary.

(Continued)

Table 7.12 (Continued)

When to Use Semicolons	
	→Suggestion: This is a place where a bulleted list would be ideal. Solves the punctuation problem and makes things very clear.
Separated with commas:	Separated with semicolons:
→Note this quotation has been modified to replace semicolons with commas (for illustrative purposes). "Since the earliest days philosophers have dreamed of a country where the mind and spirit of man would be **free,** where there would be no limits to **inquiry,** [and] where men would be free to explore the unknown and to challenge the most deeply rooted beliefs and principles."*	"Since the earliest days philosophers have dreamed of a country where the mind and spirit of man would be **free;** where there would be no limits to **inquiry;** where men would be free to explore the unknown and to challenge the most deeply rooted beliefs and principles." Justice Hugo Black, The Bill of Rights, 35 N.Y.U. L. Rev. pp. 880–81 (1960).** →Note that there is normally an "and" before the last item in a list. Since this is a quote it has been left as is.

*Justice Hugo Black, The Bill of Rights, 35 N.Y.U.L. Rev. pp. 880–81 (1960).
**Ibid.

When should you not use a semicolon? Semicolons are not used to introduce bulleted lists. They are not generally used to separate items in a list if commas are sufficient. However, if the items in the list are either long phrases or introduced with a number in parenthesis, semicolons are generally correct. Salutations are not followed with a semicolon. Table 7.13 gives examples of each of the preceding situations.

Table 7.13 Use of Semicolons

Incorrect and Correct Use of Semicolons	
Incorrect	Correct
Her tasks today include;	Her tasks today include:
• Drafting a report • Writing a memo • Organizing the meeting notes	• Drafting a report • Writing a memo • Organizing the meeting notes
→Note: By using the word "include" you have made it clear this is not a complete list. It is not necessary to say, "includes, but is not limited to" or use "and so forth" or etc.	
He will go to the park; swim; fish; and play tennis.	He will go to the park, swim, fish, and play tennis. →Note this could be a bulleted list and then no punctuation is used since the items are fragments.
Dear Mr. and Mrs. Hasselwhite;	Dear Mr. and Mrs. Hasselwhite:

Colons

Colons have four main uses. They:

- Introduce bulleted lists
- Follow a formal salutation
- Introduce subordinate lists
- Introduce subordinate sentences and clauses

Examples:

Bulleted list are almost always introduced by a colon at the end of the text preceding the first bullet: The list that introduced this topic is an example of a properly introduced bulleted list. The items are fragments so there is no period at the end.

Formal salutations are used in business correspondence (including email) and when the person to whom you are sending something is not known to you. For example:

- Dear Sir or Madam: (not "To Whom It May Concern:")
- Dear Ms. Davis:
- Dear Professor Jones:
- Dear Mr. or Ms. JK Smith:

Subordinate lists could easily be bulleted lists; instead they are kept as part of a sentence. For an example, see table 7.14.

Table 7.14 Colons and Subordinate Lists: Example

She enjoys many hobbies. Some of the more interesting ones are: quilting, rappelling, kayaking, and skydiving.

Quotation Marks

In American English, we use the paired double quotation mark (" ") when quoting someone or something or setting off words and phrases used in a nonstandard way. If there is a "quote within a quote," we use the paired single quotation mark (' ') for the internal quote.

When quoting something or someone, proper credit must be given. For short quotes, you can generally place the material in line with the text, and place quotation marks around the material. However, if you go beyond about twenty-five words, you should indent the quoted materials (generally ½" on both sides, and place it below the body text.

Using Correct Grammar and Punctuation   59

Where to place the punctuation when quotation marks are involved:

- Commas and periods go inside the right-hand quotation mark.
- Semicolons and colons go outside the right-hand quotation mark.
- Question marks and exclamation points go outside the quotation marks unless the material inside the quotation marks is a question or needs an exclamation point.
- If there is a "quote within a quote" and the quotation marks end the sentence, the period goes inside both sets of quotation marks.
- Commas go before the last word that introduces a quotation.

Apostrophes

Apostrophes have two main uses:

- Creating possessives
- Showing contractions

When creating possessives it is essential to make sure you are not confusing the possessive form with the contraction. Table 7.15 gives examples and a simple check to ensure you use the word correctly.

Table 7.15   Using Possessives and Contractions: Examples

Base Word	Possessive	Contraction	Check
It	Its	It's	Say it to yourself: It is, or its. If the correct version is "it is," you know you need "it's."
Who	Whose	Who's	Say it to yourself: Who is, or whose. If the correct version is "who is," you know you need "who's."
They/Their	Their	They're	Say it to yourself: They are, or their. If the correct version is "they are," you know you need "they're."

There are other forms of contractions worth noting. When you are leaving several letters out of a word, the convention is to use the apostrophe to indicate something is missing. For example, if you want to shorten "international," you might use "int'l." But be sure you don't use the same abbreviation for "internal" or another similar word. When you are not using the full year (2016), you should show there are numbers missing. To do this, you would place an apostrophe before the "16": '16.

Another frequently misused form of the possessive involves acronyms. If an acronym is not possessive, meaning it possesses something, it does not get an apostrophe. The classic example is the advertisement for "Joe's TV's—All

TV's are on sale this week." What is possessive about TVs? No apostrophe should be used. On the other hand, if the stands belonging to the TVs are on sale, the advertisement could read: "The TV's stand is on sale" (singular) or the TVs' stands are on sale (plural). Or you could use the avoidance technique and state "All TV stands are also on sale." Here is a table summarizing some common acronyms and examples of correct and incorrect possessives.

When you are showing possessives with a person's name, the norm is to put the apostrophe after the last letter and add the "s." If it is a single person (Charles), you add the "s" after the apostrophe. However, if the name is plural and ends in an "s" (Roberts) you don't normally add the "s"—just the apostrophe. When in doubt, style guides are very useful.

When you are writing numbers such as temperatures or years, you do not use an apostrophe unless there is something possessive about the number. For example, if you are talking about events from the 1990s, there is no apostrophe unless the event or item belongs to the 1990s. There is no apostrophe in temperatures. Table 7.16 provides some examples.

Table 7.16 Using Apostrophes: Examples

Temperatures	Correct: Temperatures today will be in the 90s.	Incorrect: Temperatures today will be in the 90's.
	Correct: 90 degrees is really warm.	Incorrect/unneeded: Ninety degrees is really warm.
Years	Correct: I really liked the '90s.	Incorrect: I really liked the 90's.
	Correct: The 1990's clothing styles were really odd.	Incorrect: The 1990s clothing styles were really odd.

→Note: When starting a sentence, bulleted item, or heading with a number, you need to spell it out. The only exception is temperatures. Better to practice avoidance, rewording the item to eliminate the problem.

Question Marks and Exclamation Points

Keep in mind that what you think is remarkable or exciting may not appear so to your readers. Instead, they may find the use of exclamation points annoying or offensive, or they may feel you are yelling at them.

Bullets

A bulleted list is almost always introduced with a colon.

Generally, the first letter of each bullet is capitalized. There are exceptions, such as when the word is not capitalized. This often happens with chemical formulas and mathematical applications.

Bullets do not require punctuation at the end unless the content of the bullet is a complete sentence. In that case, all the bullets in that list get periods, even if some are fragments.

There is no need to end each bullet with a comma or semicolon and put "and" or "or" after the last word of the next-to-last bullet and a period after the last bullet (unless it is a full sentence). If you are going to put all that punctuation in, why bother making the bulleted list in the first place? The bullets themselves imply the comma or semicolon (see table 7.17).

Table 7.17 Bullets and Punctuation

Bullets with Unnecessary Punctuation	Bullets with No Added Punctuation
At the staff meeting today we will discuss:	At the staff meeting today we will discuss:
• Employee vacation request policies; • Available and unavailable vacation days; and • Vacation swapping procedures.	• Employee vacation request policies • Available and unavailable vacation days • Vacation swapping procedures

OTHER CONSIDERATIONS

There are a few other considerations that impact the way we write, such as acronyms and highlighting.

Acronyms

Acronyms need to be created before they can be used. The only exception is acronyms that are words in their own right: IBM, SCUBA, U.S., and USA, for example.

Assuming someone "knows" an acronym can be a big mistake. After all, everyone "knows" what IT is, right? Well, maybe not. Most people will say IT = Information Technology, but in some applications, it may mean "Insurance Technology" or "Information Transfer." Better to spell this one out the first time you use it.

Organizations have many internal acronyms. Keep in mind that in today's world of electronic communications and Internet access, those acronyms go all over the place, and the recipients may not know what your acronyms mean. Or worse, they may think they know what the acronym means and come to a wrong conclusion or make a big mistake.

Think you know what an acronym stands for? Let's take a commonly used acronym that crosses many industries: NSA. Table 7.18 shows what NSA means in various industries and organizations.

Table 7.18 Why Acronyms Need to Be Spelled Out: NSA

What Does NSA Stand for?	
Intelligence Community	National Security Agency
Social Media/Dating World	No Strings Attached
Public Speaking Organizations	National Speakers Bureau
U.S. Postal Service	No Such Address
Sports	National Softball Association
Law Enforcement	National Sheriffs' Association
Accounting	National Society of Accountants
International Relations	Non-State Actor
North Atlantic Treaty Organization (NATO)	NATO Standardization Agency

If you do an Internet search, you will find there are several hundred meanings for "NSA."

This example demonstrates why if you use an acronym for one set of words, you must not use it for another set of words. If you were arranging a speaker for the NSA and hiring them from the NSA, what is really going on?

Unless you are reasonably sure your document will be split into two or more parts, acronyms should be spelled out only the first time you use them. There are two exceptions: if you have an Executive Summary or similar introductory material that managers focus on and if the acronym is used only once.

In the first case—the summary—the acronyms should be spelled out and created and then the process repeated in the body of the document.

In the second case—single use—the general rule is to not even create the acronym. However, in most business applications, this rule is not followed. For the sake of clarity, it is probably better to create the acronym even if it is used only once.

If your document is long (over twenty to thirty pages), there is a tendency to want to periodically re-create the acronym. This is not necessary, especially for electronic documents. Creating the acronym again is unneeded repetition and gives you an extra "opportunity" to introduce an error or inconsistency. When in doubt, an acronym can be a very useful addition to documents.

→Note: Proposals are often page limited. This may preclude providing an acronym list. However, many solicitation issuers allow appendices (but state they may not look at the additional material). It may be worthwhile to ask the issuer if you may provide an acronym list and not have it count against your page count.

→Tip: If you don't ask, the answer is always no.

The process of creating acronyms can dramatically impact the readability statistics, especially for short documents. There are lots of long, complicated words in the first few paragraphs of your document, and they are rendered simple by creating acronyms. When using readability, it may make sense to apply it selectively, skipping the first few paragraphs where acronyms are being created.

→Note: When starting a sentence, bulleted item, or heading with an acronym, you need to spell it out. Better to practice avoidance, rewording the sentence to eliminate the problem.

Highlighting: Bold, Italics, and Underlining

While not traditionally considered forms of punctuation, many writers use these formats to create emphasis or make a strong point. As with the exclamation point, this use may not have the effect you intended.

Web addresses auto-format into underlined text, but this is generally the only time underlining should be used.

Headings may use bold or italics, or a mix to distinguish different heading levels, but this is generally the only time they are used. The exceptions are using italics for titles of books and italics or bold on a very occasional basis to emphasize a critical or key point. Keep in mind, however, what is critical or key to you may not be to your audience. They may feel or believe you are trying to lead them to a conclusion they might not otherwise reach, and that may cause resentment or result in your document being disregarded or devalued.

NOTES

1. https://www.englishclub.com/download/english-prepositions-list.htm.
2. *Eats, Shoots & Leaves: The Zero Tolerance Approach to Punctuation*, by Lynn Truss. Profile Books Limited, November 6, 2003.
3. Ibid.

Chapter 8

Using Reader-Friendly Voice, Tone, and Person

Documents that keep the reader in mind tend to get much better responses and results than documents that are written for the author or the author's manager or supervisor. Here are several more tools you can use to create reader-friendly documents:

- Voice
- Tone
- Person

These three elements combine to create both your and your organization's brand.

VOICE

Voice generally refers to passive or active voice, but can also refer to your "corporate" or "organizational" voice. The more active the voice you use the more likely your reader will see him or herself in the document and view the document as requiring action or a response.

Corporate or organizational documents reflect the culture of the entity and are often written to be very general, without targeting a specific audience. The target is generally broad: people seeking mortgages, or families planning a ski vacation, or sailing enthusiasts. The writer must follow organizational guidelines and doesn't really know the specifics about the audience. The end result is a document generally written in passive voice.

But voice is much more than the mechanics of grammar. "Voice" is what makes what you write yours—it reflects your (or the company's) point of view, personality, or style.

When you know your target audience, you are able to write in a more engaging, inviting style, often using active voice to draw your reader into your document.

A strong voice helps you make every word count, establishes consistency across your website or body of work, and most importantly helps you grab your readers' attention and establish a relationship with them.[1]

TONE

Tone is not the same as "voice." Your tone is set through word choices, mix of active and passive voice, and type of audience. You may choose words that are simple and lighthearted but set them in a story or report that is very serious to keep from overwhelming your audience.

Tone often is set by the degree of formality of your document. Table 8.1 contrasts words that are formal versus words that are informal.

Table 8.1 Formal versus Informal Word Choices

Informal Word Choices and Style Are:	Formal Word Choices and Style Are:
Plain, simple	Ornate, complicated
Humorous, light-hearted	Serious, proper
Casual, informal	Formal, rigid
Contractions	Spelled-out words

The words in this table are both word choices you might make in your documents and verbs describing how you might set the tone of your writing. Often, your tone and word choices are mandated by organizational policy, goals, and culture.

PERSON

The "person" you use in your writing is often dictated by the audience, organizational policy, and management requirements. Writing entirely in third person (he/she/it, him/her, they/them/their, and organization name) can come across as very stilted and stuffy. It is often hard to read. It doesn't encourage the readers to see any roles for them in the goals of your document.

Many corporate documents need to be written in the third person. This is particularly true of many reports, plans, and similar documents. Three major exceptions are websites, marketing materials, and proposals.

Websites are designed and written to appeal to a broad market—the general public and specific users. To achieve this goal, the website is often written in simple, concise, easy-to-read language—plain English. The text is often in first and second person ("We want you to do XYZ."). If the website is written mostly in third person, the reader may not see any value to filling his or her goals. The website is not enticing or engaging. Solution providers and problem solvers write about their products and services in the first and second person. Information conveyers tend to use the third person.

Marketing materials, in addition to electronic content, are also generally written in the first and second person. You want the person or organization to buy from you, so you need to write in a voice that engages the reader and makes him or her see themselves as a possible buyer and your organization as their seller of choice.

Proposals to provide goods or services are often written in the first and second person. You want the reviewer to envision your organization as the provider of the products or services being sought. Third person may not accomplish this goal.

→Tip: It is fine to mix first, second, and third person. In fact, this can be an excellent approach when writing proposals.

NOTE

1. http://www.quickanddirtytips.com/education/grammar/understanding-voice-and-tone-in-writing?page=all.

Chapter 9

Applying Effective Self-Editing and Self-Proofreading Techniques

SELF-EDITING

If you have the services of an editor available, you are very fortunate. Most people have to be their own editors, deal with the input of management, or rely on colleagues to provide this service. It is very difficult to edit your own work. If you liked something the first time you read it, and you didn't find any problems, you will like it even better the next time you read it . . . but it will be just as wrong.

So, how do you function as your own editor?

There are a number of process-based or formulaic approaches to use when you must be your own editor. The most common technique is to let your material "rest" for several hours or longer, and then reread it. However, this may not be feasible, given time constraints, and you are still likely to overlook things that a formulaic approach will find.

So, what does "formulaic approach" mean?

There are a number of small actions you can take that will fix basic inconsistencies and errors in your documents. The process also enables you to use your peripheral vision to spot other issues. Looking straight at something is often not the best way to spot something—instead, looking out the "corner of your eye" enables you to see things that are otherwise not obvious.

So, how does it work?

1. Start with a simple find/replace: Search for "space-space" (using the spacebar twice) and replace all with "space" (again using the spacebar, but one time). This will replace all instances of two spaces in your document. Then, repeat the process since many people have "slippery fingers" and

may have three (or more) spaces in some places. Repeat until there are no more instances of two spaces.

→Note that if you use the spacebar to position things, this will completely mess up that "formatting." Better to get into the habit of using the "Tab" key, page layout features, and paragraph formatting features to align text.

2. Search your document for words that you know you have problems with: principle/principal; accept/except; alternate/alternative; use/utilize; and preventive/preventative as examples. Look carefully at how you intended the word to be used and change or modify as necessary. In the process of doing this, you will often see other issues—out of the corner of your eye.

→If you are not sure how to use a word, or if the grammatical niceties are escaping you, go for avoidance. Avoidance is a great technique to both self-edit and deal with problem structures or words. It also makes your writing more interesting since you have to put some thought into how to avoid a complex or confusing situation.

3. Look for acronyms that have been created more than once, not created the first time, or not created the first time but instead later in the document (second or subsequent use). The first and last situations are very common with multiauthor documents and documents where someone in the review cycle adds text without checking on the acronym use and creation.

→How do you search for acronyms to ensure they have been properly created? There are several ways. A reliable way is to search the document for all the acronyms, make a list, and then go back through to make sure they were created at first use and not later or more than once. If you don't see the acronym created—it has just "appeared"—you need to take the least common word in the acronym and search the document for that word. Each time the chosen word appears, examine the text to see if that should be the first use of the acronym. Then create it. Continue the search to ensure the phrase associated with the acronym doesn't appear elsewhere in the document. If it does, you can replace the phrase with the acronym. During this process, you will often spot other issues during your searches.

4. Look for long sentences. If you see lots of commas, you probably have a bulleted list asking to be let out. Or, you may have a run-on sentence or a sentence that can have words removed or be split into two or more sentences. Again, you will find other issues while doing this and be creating a reader- or audience-friendly document.

5. Look for long paragraphs. If your paragraphs routinely run to more than six sentences (especially if the sentences routinely exceed fifteen words), you probably can make two or more paragraphs. Even more issues will probably surface during this process.
6. If you have a tendency to put commas and periods outside the right-hand quotation mark, you can do another find/replace. In this instance, you can search for," and replace with,." and repeat for the period.

This is far from an exhaustive list of the formulaic approaches you can use to self-editing. If you combine these simple steps with your own techniques and follow them with a careful rereading of your document (after a few hours away), you will find most of the issues. At this point, it would be very beneficial to ask someone to read through your document to flag inconsistencies and areas of confusion.

When you ask for assistance with editing or proofreading your document, make sure you are asking for the correct service.

Proofreading is done at the very end of the document production cycle. A proofreader is only supposed to look for typos, formatting issues, incorrect word usage, spelling errors, and punctuation errors.

If you are fortunate enough to have an editor, here's what you should normally expect. Editors often do all of the proofreader tasks, plus a whole lot more. They look for flow, logic, suitability of headings, and completeness of overall content. They also move material around and remove duplicate material. They may append lots of comments for the author to explain their editing rationale or ask for author or subject matter expert clarification.

Editing should happen after the first draft of your document is done and, then, after the first round of revisions is made. Only after the final edits have been reconciled and all the changes and comments dealt with should a document go to the proofreader (if the editor did not provide that service).

STYLE GUIDES

There are dozens of style guides in print and on the Internet. Some of the main ones are as follows:

- *The Associated Press Stylebook* (*AP Stylebook*), 2015
- *Chicago Manual of Style*, sixteenth edition
- your organization's style guide
- U.S. Government Printing Office (GPO) style manual
- *Elements of Style*: A classic reference that every writer should use
- *Publication Manual of the American Psychological Association* (APA), sixth edition

At work, you are most likely to use the *AP Stylebook* or the *Chicago Manual of Style*, or a mix of the two. The *AP Stylebook* is intended for journalistic writing so it is well suited to marketing materials, website content, articles, newsletters, and other short, less formal documents. The *Chicago Manual of Style* is more likely to be used for reports, studies, plans, and proposals. Two other guides you may use are the APA guide and the GPO guide. The APA guide is used for dissertations and theses and the GPO guide for correct use of terminology and spelling/capitalization for Federal Government applications.

The main differences and key similarities between the *AP Stylebook* and the *Chicago Manual of Style* are summarized in table 9.1.

Table 9.1 Comparison of AP Stylebook and Chicago Manual of Style

AP Stylebook	*Chicago Manual of Style*
Key Similarities	
One space after all punctuation, including periods	
Comma before "and" in a list of like things unless its use makes the meaning unclear	
Internet, not internet; intranet, not Intranet; website, not Web site or Website; Web for Worldwide Web	
Main Differences	
Hyphenation to create compound words is inconsistent:	Hyphenation to create compound words is inconsistent:
• Carry-over • Login • Playoff • Rundown	• Carryover • Log-in • Play-off • Rundown (n.) • Run-down (adj.)
Use numerals for numbers 10 and above; exception is for measurements—these numbers are not spelled out.	Spell out numbers up to 99 (ninety-nine); exception is for measurements—these numbers are not spelled out.
Book titles in quotation marks	Book titles in italics

→Buying style guides is expensive, and they are continually being updated. Rather than spend money on something so fluid, take a few minutes to get a library card. The style guides would be available in your library and are almost certain to be up-to-date.

Chapter 10

Netiquette and Writing for the Likely Viewing Medium

Almost anything you write is likely to end up "out there" courtesy of the ease of information flow via the Internet. In the old days, letters were written employing the basics of etiquette; today, emails and other electronic communications employ the provisions of Internet + Etiquette, or "Netiquette." Very little of what organizations write is kept in paper format. Even if classified, the information is available to authorized users via electronic means such as an intranet.

→Note: Capitalization for Internet and intranet . . . Internet is a proper noun (and there is only one Internet) so it is capitalized; intranet is not a proper noun (there are many intranets out there) so it is not capitalized. If you are referring to a particular, named intranet, the term could be capitalized as part of the name: The XYZ Company Intranet.

Since what you write is very likely to end up on the Internet, or at least on one or more intranets, it is essential to consider a few things:

- Who is likely to access the information?
- What will they access the information for?
- Is the information clear, concise, complete, and current?
- Could the information be readily misconstrued, especially if taken out of context?
- What medium or media would most likely be used to view the material?
- Will the viewer have access to high throughput (bandwidth or data rate) links to download large files, graphics, and so forth?
- For email: Is the subject clear and compelling? Is the key information addressed in the first two lines of the email? Are the language and structure considerate?

- For social media: Is the information you are posting potentially exposing the organization or company to risks? Could the position in the posting be considered as representing the views or position of the company or organization?

A BRIEF HISTORY OF THE EVOLUTION OF THE INTERNET

The Internet, as we know it, evolved from humble origins in the 1960s (the ARPANET) when it was a system allowing quick communications between scientists, university researchers, and government staff to a system expanded by the Defense Advanced Research Projects Agency (DARPA), to a decentralized electronic communications system that is transparent to the user—the Internet. The concept behind the Internet involves many elements including packet-switching technology, dispersed servers, and distributed communications to increase security. Since data across the Internet travels at the speed of light, it can circle the globe approximately 7.5 times in one second. This means email messages can be divided into "packets" of data and sent by numerous paths, through various servers, circle the globe several times, be reassembled at the receiving end, and appear in your inbox in less than one second.

But the most important thing when it comes to written communications is that the Internet works.

A FEW IMPORTANT CONSIDERATIONS FOR INTERNET COMMUNICATIONS

When you send something over the Internet, the communication takes on a life of its own. Here are a few things to keep in mind:

- Email never dies. It can be forwarded, stored, or otherwise archived. It can be deleted from your computer . . . but approximately 90 percent of anything that was ever on your computer can be recovered even if it has been deleted or written over.
- Your email goes through approximately twenty servers worldwide. Some of those servers are in places where they may not like us and others are with competitors who would like to get their hands on your data. You have little to no control over how your packetized message is routed once you hit "send."
- The "recall" feature doesn't work very well, if it works at all. There may be a window of a few seconds when you can recall a message, but it is not something you should rely upon.

- Consider the medium your email is most likely to be viewed on. Probably a mobile device. Often, while someone is rushing through an airport or heading to a meeting. If they can't see what's important on the initial screen, your message may not be read or acted upon until much later, if at all.

EMAIL AND TEXT MESSAGING FAUX PAS

Email is easy. Just type, hit send, and forget about it. Not really. The ease of using email is one of its biggest benefits and worst shortcomings.

Here is a partial list of common email mistakes:

- Subject lines that are not relevant, accurate, or compelling
- Sloppy typing (think autocorrect and what it can do!)
- Using jargon and emoticons
- Including taglines or quotes
- Using all capital letters
- Using all lowercase letters
- Reply all
- Using all "to" or "cc" addressees
- Not putting the most critical information in the first two lines
- Emailing in anger or frustration

The Subject Line

Your subject line needs to immediately convey the topic of your email. You may even indicate there are attachments in the email. Poor subject lines can result in your email being diverted to spam. Some servers strip off attachments, so telling the recipient there are attachments as part of the subject line may be very useful. Make sure you are avoiding words like "special," or "free," or "guaranteed" that spam filters key on.

Sloppy Typing

Sloppy typing, and its sibling, social media shorthand, can cause serious problems. You may think you typed "compliant" but actually typed "complaint." This may cause frustration, or even anger, on the part of the recipient. Other instances of sloppy typing can be even more serious. Maybe you want someone to meet you in the "hall," but you were in a hurry and typed "h*ll." This is not the way to win friends or influence people. Text messages can be even more problematic since most people use autocorrect and what gets sent is not even close to what you intended. Always make a minute to review before sending. In the case of email, consider typing the message off line and then dropping the text into the message.

→Tip: Don't put the addressees or subject in your email until after you have typed and reviewed the text. You should be prompted several times to complete these fields before the message goes out. If you are angry, this feature may save you a lot of embarrassment (or worse).

Jargon and Emoticons

These items have little or no place in business and professional writing. What you find amusing may not be viewed in the same way by your audience. To make matters worse, the recipients may forward your email or text to others who have even less appreciation for your sense of humor or no understanding of your jargon.

Taglines and Quotes

You may have a quote, Bible verse, or other tagline you really like. Unfortunately, your known (and unintended) recipients may not share your interests or beliefs. Even something as seeming innocuous as an Einstein or Eleanor Roosevelt quote may upset some people.

Capital Letters

Typing in all capital letters accomplishes two things—neither being what you had in mind. First, many people view this as shouting. People don't like to be yelled at. Second, it shows laziness. These are not actions designed to impress recipients.

→Note: Subject lines of emails should be in title case.

Lowercase Letters

As with using all capital letters, using all lowercase letters shows laziness. It also shows a lack of respect for the recipient since you are not even capitalizing the person's name.

Reply All

It is tempting to use "reply all" when confirming attendance at a meeting, or receipt of information, or when you need to reply to several of the email recipients. But it is not a good idea. When fifty people each reply to fifty other people and then some of those reply to all fifty again, and so forth, you can quickly bog down your server and intranet. In addition, using "reply all" is a form of laziness and can really annoy some people.

Choosing Addressees

Ever wonder how you get on so many spammers' and businesses' email lists? It may have something to do with the use of "to" and "cc" when "bcc" might have been more appropriate. If you are sending out a company-wide email, why not use "bcc" and indicate in the body of the email that the entire company received a copy? This approach precludes someone forwarding the email, with its entire addressee list, to an unintended recipient.

Using "cc" to show the "to" addressees you have included managers or other colleagues in the mailing can backfire. Some people get offended—they feel you are informing on them or something similar. Of course, using "bcc" does the same thing, but it could be problematic if the "to" or "cc" addressees find out from a "bcc" addressee that you were not up front about the recipients.

Make the Critical Information Visible

If the reader can't see the key information in the first two lines, there is a possibility that he or she may miss something like attachments or deadlines or meeting locations. It is best to assume someone will initially read your email on a smart phone or similar small-screen device.

Emailing or Texting in Anger or Frustration

You've probably both emailed (and texted) when you were angry or upset and received emails and texts from others who were angry. Unfortunately, once sent, the likelihood of recovering the message unread is slim. These messages take on a life of their own. Better to let the email or text rest for an hour before sending it. Even better, don't put in the recipients, or create the email or text offline, or make it a draft. These are all ways to vent your anger or frustration without sending something you may later regret.

Social Media Faux Pas

Using social media is fraught with risks. From a business perspective, anything you put out on social media can potentially be construed as representing the position of your employer. Many things you put out there can be accessed by potential employers, people who don't like you, and criminals, among others.

As with email and text messaging, social media writing is filled with sloppy typing and error-filled data, thanks to autocorrect.

Unless you are part of the company public relations or marketing staff, social media is something you probably should not use in a work context, and it is something to use with care in a personal context.

Conclusion
The Wrap-Up

Writing in plain English—using plain language—is the surest way to get your intended meaning across to the widest possible audience. Your readers will thank you for making your materials the ones they can follow. You will be far more likely to get the results you want and need. You will become the go-to resource because your stuff is clear and concise and follows the KISS principle.

Writing in plain language is not always easy. It takes time and effort . . . but the end result is worthwhile.

For the record, the readability statistics for this book are as follows:

- Reading ease: 57.3
- Grade level: 9.0
- Passive sentences: 13 percent

About the Author

Janet Arrowood has been a writer, technical editor, and writing trainer for over thirty-five years. Ms. Arrowood is a mathematician by degree, an engineer by training, and a writer by profession. She specializes in training professionals to write in "plain English"; proposal and grant writing and training; writing government and military communications; technical and professional writing; and presentation skills training. She has worked with numerous government agencies and clients throughout the world including:

- U.S. Office of Personnel Management (OPM)
- NASA Goddard Space Flight Center (GSFC)
- Consumer Financial Protection Bureau (CFPB)
- Environmental Protection Agency (EPA) Ecosystems Research Division (ERD)
- U.S. Department of Energy National Renewable Energy Laboratory (NREL)
- U.S. Department of Commerce Institute for Telecommunication Sciences (ITS)
- National Science Foundation University Corporation/National Center for Atmospheric Research (UCAR/NCAR)
- Colorado Office of Economic Development and International Trade
- Colorado Department of Transportation
- North Atlantic Treaty Organization (NATO)
- United Nations Organizations (UNEP, UNDP, UNOPS)
- Global Environmental Facility (GEF)
- Secretariat of the South Pacific Regional Environmental Program (SPREP)
- Regional Transportation District (Denver)

- UniGroup
- Herzog Contracting Corporation
- Newmont Mining, Freeport-McMoRan International (FMI)
- Knight Piésold
- Mountain States Employers Council

In addition to her training, editing, and writing expertise, Janet brings both engineering and military backgrounds to her work. She served as an Army Signal Corps Officer, a member of the technical staff at MITRE, and a staff engineer at Martin Marietta and NATO. She holds a degree in mathematics from Vanderbilt University and has completed graduate-level courses in operations research at George Washington University. Janet's "plain language" programs are consistently rated among the highest in any organization where she facilitates training.

Janet Arrowood founded The Write Source, Inc. (www.TheWriteSourceInc.com), a woman- and veteran-owned small business, in 1993. She can be reached at Janet.C.Arrowood@gmail.com.

www.ingramcontent.com/pod-product-compliance
Lightning Source LLC
Chambersburg PA
CBHW021215240426
43672CB00026B/323